TWO LITTLE OLD LADIES

LADIES

IT'S ALL IN THE ATTITUDE

Written by Susan York Meyers
Illustrations by Acacia A. Anthis

Doodle and Peck Publishing
Yukon, Oklahoma

Doodle and Peck Publishing
P. O. Box 852105
Yukon, OK 73085
www.doodleandpeck.com

Publisher's Note: This is a work of fiction. Names, characters, places, and incidents are a product of the author's imagination. Locales and public names are sometimes used for atmospheric purposes. Any resemblance to actual people, living or dead, or to businesses, companies, events, institutions, or locales is completely coincidental.

All Bible scripture references are taken from The New International Version.

Library of Congress Control Number: 2015950586

Book Layout and Cover Art: Marla F. Jones

Ordering Information:
Quantity sales. Special discounts are available on quantity purchases by corporations, associations, and others. For details, contact the Sales Department at the address above.

Two Little Old Ladies/Susan York Meyers-- 1st ed.
ISBN 978-0-9966205-0-5

Dedicated to Robin, my accomplice for several of the adventures in this book, and to my publisher, Marla, who believes in Lillybelle and Annabelle as much as I do.

Resolutions made
On the eve of a new year
Same old, same old

CHAPTER ONE

Borrowing Trouble

"We're going to be late getting to the Shady Rest Nursing Home," Lillybelle stated. She climbed into the passenger side of the VW van in her most ladylike manner. "What a name for a nursing home. It would look better on the front gate of a cemetery."

Annabelle settled into the driver's seat. Her gold bangle bracelets jingled softly as she started the van then carefully backed it onto the road. "So you always say. Anyway, we should be on time. Although it is later than I thought."

Lillybelle straightened her gray pillbox hat. "Of course it is. You never pay attention to the time. I have to admit, though, your idea for Wilma's gift was perfect. The only pictures taken at her wedding were those tiny Polaroids. Getting one blown up, matted and framed was inspired. Turn left here."

"I know where to turn." Annabelle peered down the street. "There's the frame shop."

"Hurry and get parked. Better yet, just pull up and let me out. I'll go in and pay while you circle the block. If we're late, Wilma might go down for a nap before we get to give her our gift."

Annabelle came to a stop in front of Peters' Perfect Fit Framers. "At ninety-five, she should get to nap whenever she wants. See you in a bit."

Lillybelle slid out of the van, one hand holding her hat, the other making sure her knee length gray and white striped skirt stayed in place.

Annabelle hummed as she drove the tree-lined block. Three turns later, she found herself back on Richmond Street. Lillybelle stood on the sidewalk in front of the framers.

"Where's the picture?" Annabelle asked as her sister got into the van.

"We're too early," Lillybelle replied. "It's not done yet. According to Mr. Peters, he told us 3:00. It's only 2:30."

"Well, I don't want to wait in front of the store for a half hour," Annabelle mused. "I know! Let's try that new cupcake shop on Elm."

"We're going to eat cake in an hour," Lillybelle reminded her.
"So?"

Lillybelle waved in the direction of the street. "Good point. Drive on."

After a few twists and turns, the Angels and Roses Tearoom appeared, tucked behind a beautifully landscaped yard filled with angel statues and rosebushes.

"This is darling," Annabelle exclaimed as they exited the van. "Don't you just love the smell of roses?"

"We need to hurry," Lillybelle said. "Otherwise we'll be late picking up the picture."

"Of course, Sister, you're right. I wonder if we can sit at one of those darling little ice cream parlor tables on the patio?"

A couple of delicious cupcakes later, Annabelle slid behind the wheel of the van and asked, "Now, should I take a left or a right?"

"How should I know? You're the driver."

"Hah, don't stop backseat driving now, Sister. Maybe it was left."

"We are going to be sooo late," Lillybelle moaned. "Go left, now right, right again, one more right."

"We're back on Elm. Wave at the nice police officer."

"Okay, go left, another left, now another," Lillybelle ordered. "It's got to be this street."

"Nope, still Elm. Just a different corner. See, there's that nice police officer walking down the block. He's grinning."

Lillybelle straightened her hat, a determined look coming into her eyes. "Okay, go ahead two blocks. Now, take a left, another left, now right."

"There's the policeman again. He's waving us down." Annabelle pulled slowly to the side of the street.

"Oh, dear, do you suppose he thinks we're terrorists?"

"What would we be terrorizing, Sister?" Annabelle inquired. "The yarn store or the doggie groomer?"

When Lillybelle rolled down her window, the patrolman asked, "Ladies, are you lost?"

Annabelle leaned over. "I'm afraid so. Do you know where Peters' Perfect Fit Framers is?"

"Two blocks straight back," he said.

"Oh my, how did we end up back on Richmond?" she exclaimed. "Thank you, Officer."

"Yes, thank you," Lillybelle added.

A couple of minutes later, Lillybelle pointed. "There's the shop. And there's an open parking place right in front. I'll just be a minute."

True to her word, Lillybelle hurried. "Now," she said as she rejoined Annabelle, "we have the picture and we can just make it to the party before Wilma takes out her teeth. I really don't want to watch her gumming chocolate cake."

"Sister…"

"What now?" Lillybelle asked.

"Aren't we supposed to bring the cake?"

Lillybelle sighed. "Take a right at the stoplight."

§

"You know," Lillybelle mused after they'd retrieved the cake. "If we hadn't been so worried about being late, we would have been on time."

"True," Annabelle agreed. "We'd have gotten to the framing store at 3:00, not gone to the cupcake shop and never gotten lost. All this trouble caused by needless worrying."

"So, should we be worried that Wilma has her teeth out?"

"No, Sister. From now on, we'll borrow sugar, not trouble."

"A good attitude to take," Lillybelle agreed.

§

A Thought . . . The next time you find yourself perusing your list of worries, get down on your knees. That's the wonderful thing about God – He's always available. Let Him cross the worries off your list.

A Scripture . . . Who of you by worrying can add a single hour to your life? ~ Luke 12:25

And a Prayer . . . Dear Father, it seems that if I can worry about it, I will. But even though half of the stuff I worry about never comes to pass, it doesn't stop me from wringing my hands and trying to solve all my problems. Even the ones that haven't happened yet. I pray for the courage to "let go and let you." In Jesus' name, Amen

What's worse than biting
Into a rotten apple?
Finding half a worm!

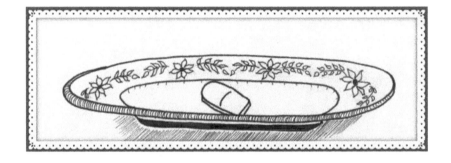

CHAPTER TWO

Talking About Food

"Too much starch," Lillybelle stated as she peered over her sister's shoulder.

Annabelle looked at the baking potatoes she'd been scrubbing then frowned at her sister. "I beg your pardon?"

"Potatoes are full of starch. It's not good for you." Lillybelle smoothed the front of her blue slacks and sat down at the kitchen table.

"I suppose you're right, Sister. How about a nice salad instead?"

"You bought iceberg lettuce. It has no real nutritional value. You need the dark green, leafy stuff."

"Hmm," Annabelle replied thoughtfully. She walked over and peered into the refrigerator. "I could warm up the soup."

"You added the leftover hamburger meat to it. Too much grease." Lillybelle tapped her finger on the yellow Formica tabletop for emphasis. "Sister, we do need to eat better!"

"I agree," Annabelle replied. "But don't you think we could try moderation instead of giving up *all* food?"

Lillybelle sniffed. "That's the problem with folks today. They want to do things half-way. If you are going to do something, you need to it right."

"I see. I guess I could make us a healthy fruit salad."

But a firm headshake greeted this suggestion. "Eat too much fruit, and it's just like eating sugar."

Annabelle pushed a strand of long silver hair behind her ear and inquired, "Eggs?"

"Cholesterol."

Annabelle sighed. "Assuming I find something we *can* eat, will you brew the tea?"

"You have heard of caffeine, haven't you?"

"Let me see what I can do," Annabelle said. A few minutes later, she placed a plate in front of her sister.

"What in the world is this?" Lillybelle demanded. She pushed at it with her pinky.

"It's a multivitamin. It's all I have left in the kitchen. It's that or the cat food. Enjoy!"

"On second thought," Lillybelle said slowly, "maybe moderation is the key. I'll have a small salad, a cup of soup, a boiled egg, a glass of tea, a small baked potato, and some fruit for dessert."

Annabelle stared at her.

"And maybe I'll get up and help you make it," Lillybelle added.

"Now you're talking sense," Annabelle replied.

§

A Thought. . . It's easy to get caught up in a new idea. But sometimes we need to ask ourselves, "Am I going overboard?" Sometimes little changes are easier to stick to than an attempt at one big swooping change that almost guarantees failure.

A Scripture... *Be diligent in these matters; give yourself wholly to them, so that everyone may see your progress.* ~ I Timothy 4:15

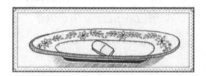

And a prayer... Father, help me to remember that moderation is often the key. Prayerful baby steps are often the best way to success. In Jesus' name, Amen

Creative merging
Of the mind and emotion
And wonder achieved

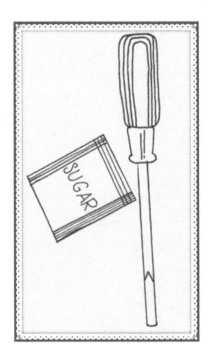

CHAPTER THREE

Fixing A Table

"This table is wobbly," Lillybelle remarked.

Annabelle joined her sister at the kitchen table. "Stick a sugar packet under it."

Lillybelle frowned. "That's not fixing the problem. That's ignoring it."

"So, what do you propose we do?" Annabelle inquired as she took a sip of tea.

Lillybelle absently played with her strand of pearls while she thought. "We could call someone."

"For a wobbly table leg?"

Lillybelle frowned. "Hmm, I see your point. Do you know where the screwdriver is?"

"I believe it's in the shed. I'll check after I finish my tea."

A half hour later, Lillybelle went in search of her sister. "Have you found the screwdriver?" she asked.

"No, but I admit, I got distracted." Annabelle sat cross-legged on the shed floor, her long ribbon skirt pooled around her.

"You'll never be able to get up from that position. What are you doing?"

"Sorting bulbs. It will be planting season soon. And yes, I'll be able to get back up. That's what yoga is for." She sniffed the bulb she held in her hands. "I just love the smell of dirt. It makes me think of summer."

"Good to know." Lillybelle snorted. "I'll put some in a box for your birthday. It'll be much cheaper than perfume. Now, will you help me look for the screwdriver?"

A search of the shed yielded a lost rake, but no screwdriver.

"You know," Lillybelle mused, "I may have used it to tighten the plant hangers on the back porch. I'll bet that's where it is."

"I'll put these bulbs away and join you in a minute." Not much later, Annabelle stood on the back porch and stripped off her gardening gloves. "The bulbs are ready for planting. Did you find the screwdriver?"

Lillybelle shook her head. "No. In fact, I've been straightening the gardening table. I've stacked these clay pots in order from smallest to largest. See how much space we have now."

"Sister, after all this work, I think we deserve a cup of tea."

"That does sound nice."

Back in their cozy kitchen, Annabelle poured them both a cup of orange spice tea.

Lillybelle reached out and jiggled the table. It didn't move. "How did you fix it?"

"I stuck a sugar packet under the leg."

Lillybelle shrugged. "Well, I guess productive is productive. And we were certainly productive today. Maybe we'll find the screwdriver tomorrow."

"Maybe we will, Sister," murmured Annabelle. "Maybe we will."

A Thought... Days don't always bring what we think they will. Sometimes goals should be reevaluated, accomplishments redefined. *Sometimes* we need to give ourselves a break.

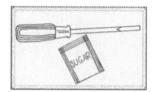

A Scripture... *Now finish the work, so that your eager willingness to do it may be matched by your completion of it, according to your means.* 2 Corinthians 8:11

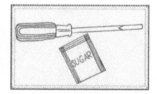

And a prayer... Dear Father, I know it's easy to make excuses. Help me instead to achieve. Even though it might be just one small task, help me to work toward the goal. In Jesus' name, Amen

Wiggly fat bare toes
Squiggly worms after a rain
Made for a mud hole

CHAPTER FOUR

Making Mud Pies

"Spring is wet," Lillybelle huffed. She gazed out the front window and patted her newly set gray hair. "And when things are wet, people should stay inside."

"Who's outside?" Annabelle asked. She joined her sister at the window. "Oh, look at all the fun the Waynesboro children are having splashing in the puddles." She clapped her hands together causing her bangle bracelets to jingle. "I wonder if they'd like some ginger cookies." With a swish of her skirt she hurried toward the kitchen.

A moment later she headed outside with a filled plate. "You look like you're having fun," Annabelle told the two little girls sitting in the mud. "Would you like some cookies?"

The blonde with the flyaway hair grinned. "Thanks. We're making mud pies."

"May I join you?" Annabelle asked.

"Sure," a curly-haired moppet replied.

Annabelle sat on the grass, took a deep breath, and shoved both hands in the mud. She grabbed two squishy handfuls. First she made it into a ball then, splat, smashed the ball into a flat circle.

But something didn't seem right. She peered at the girls. Ah, that was it. Annabelle eased off her silver sandals. She slipped her toes into the mud and wiggled. Wonderful!

Inside the house, Lillybelle peeked out the window. Did her sister really have her feet in the mud? "She's crazy," Lillybelle told the cat.

Primrose licked her white paws in agreement. Tramping around in the mud was more than she could imagine anyone wanting to do.

Lillybelle pushed her glasses back on her nose and squinted for a better view. "We'll be lucky if the neighbors don't call the loony bin. But she does look like she's having fun."

Lillybelle donned a scarf to protect her hair and rain boots to protect her feet then made her way across the lawn to the mud-splattered trio. "You do realize you are playing in my flower garden."

"Oh, fiddle," Annabelle replied. "Nothing's planted here yet."

The two rag-a-muffins grinned.

"Carly! Charlotte!" a voice called. "Time for lunch."

The children hurried to their feet.

"Thank you for playing with us," Carly said.

"You make wonderful mud pies," Charlotte called over her shoulder.

"Thank you, my dears," Annabelle replied.

"You don't look very grown up," Lillybelle said.

"I don't feel very grown up." Annabelle held out a perfectly round mud pie. "Do you think it needs more grass on top?"

A smile played at Lillybelle's mouth. "No, I think it has just the right amount." She sat beside her sister. "How can you stand to have your feet in that stuff?"

Annabelle wiggled her toes and laughed. "You should try it."

Lillybelle took off her rain boots. She slipped off her proper shoes and peeled off her knee-hi stockings. Gingerly, she dipped her toes in the mud, then shoved her feet in right up to the ankles.

"Being grown up is overrated?" Annabelle asked.

"Sometimes," Lillybelle said around a giggle, "it is."

A Thought... God has given us a world in which to live, a redeemer to save us, and joy beyond measure. Enjoy! ~Mischelle Creager

A Scripture... *"The joy of the Lord is your strength."* Nehemiah 8:10b

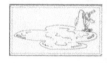

And a Prayer... Lord, help me find joy in the life you've given me. Teach me when to be serious and when to laugh. Your word tells me there's a time for both. In Jesus' name, Amen

Now the Lord whispers
Fills the well of my soul with
His abiding love

CHAPTER FIVE

Giving A Little Comfort

"**W**ords are never enough," Lillybelle commented. Grabbing a crocheted potholder, she took her famous tuna casserole out of the oven.

"No," Annabelle agreed, "words are never enough. But they're all we have." She smoothed plastic wrap around a plate of ginger cookies. "Do you realize Jack and Vivian were married fifty-six years?"

"I know. They were true life-mates. The preacher's wife is going over to Vivian's house," Lillybelle mused. "We could take our food over to the church. Annie would be glad to deliver it, and that would mean fewer visitors for Vivian to cope with."

"You're right, Sister." Annabelle's long skirt swished as she searched for the car keys.

"They're on the hook where they should be," Lillybelle told her. "I drove last."

In the van, the sisters were silent for a few blocks. Then Lillybelle remarked, "Too many people gathering around can be overwhelming during a time of grief. It might be a blessing to Vivian for us to forgo stopping by."

"True." Annabelle maneuvered their small van around a pothole. "There's Annie's car in front of the church."

"What's our decision?" Lillybelle asked. "Do we leave the food with Annie or drive to Vivian's house?"

Annabelle sighed. "Friends don't always know the right thing to say..."

"...but they're always there," Lillybelle finished.

A few minutes later, Lillybelle rang Vivian's doorbell. When she answered, both sisters hugged their dear friend.

"We are so sorry," Annabelle whispered. "So very sorry."

A Thought... It's not how you say you're sorry, or the delicious food you bring that people will remember. It's you. That you acknowledged their loss. That you cared.

A Scripture... Shout for joy, you heavens; rejoice, you earth; burst into song, you mountains! For the Lord comforts his people and will have compassion on his afflicted ones. ~ Isaiah 49:13

And a Prayer... Dear Father, when a friend is hurting, help me to be a comfort. And help me to remember You will take it from there. In Jesus' name, Amen

Sneaker practical
Deep inside she's a vision
In high-heeled red shoes

CHAPTER SIX

Going To the Beauty Parlor

"Myrtle's running behind," Annabelle told Lillybelle. She settled onto the patchwork couch next to the washing machine.

"Isn't she always? Sometimes I think we should consider frequenting a stylist who doesn't work out of her garage/laundry room/salon." Lillybelle flicked a piece of lint off her flowered blouse.

Across the garage/laundry room/salon, Myrtle worked on a client. Annabelle smiled. "It would break Myrtle's heart if we stopped coming here. At least she took down the basketball hoop from the garage door."

"Thank goodness! I was hearing 'thump, thump, thump' in my sleep."

"What are you having done today?" Annabelle asked.

Lillybelle stared at her. "Why, the same style I've been getting for the last twenty-five years, Sister."

"Of course."

"What do you mean, 'of course'? The last time you changed *your* hair, phones still had dials." Lillybelle reached over and pointed at the hairstyle gracing a magazine cover. "Maybe you're thinking about something like that?"

Annabelle studied the black and white mohawk. "It's a little too fancy for Ladies' Bible Class, don't you think?"

"I do."

The bell tinkled. A woman strode in and informed Myrtle, "I've got an appointment."

"I'm running a little late," Myrtle replied around the pink clip in her mouth. "Have a seat."

The woman hesitated. She glanced over her shoulder then nodded. Settling into a folding chair, she immediately pulled out a phone and began typing.

"What's she doing?" Lillybelle whispered. "She's not making a call."

"Believe it or not, Sister, new phones can connect to the internet," Annabelle replied. "They're called smart phones." She peered at the woman from under her eyelashes. "Don't you just love it?"

"Love what?" Lillybelle inquired. She plucked a used laundry sheet off her sleeve and deposited it into the trash.

"That woman's hair."

Lillybelle squinted in the woman's direction. "It's got a purple streak in it."

"Isn't it marvelous? Do you think I could pull that off?"

"At your age?"

"Why not?" Annabelle ran her fingers through her long, silvery hair.

Lillybelle touched her own artfully styled gray waves. "You're the one who always says she wants to be completely natural."

"Yes, well, one must be open to change, and I like that purple! Where do you think she's going after this? A swanky party? Or maybe a clandestine rendezvous?"

"If she's that type, why is she getting her hair done at Myrtle's House of Style?"

"Sister, it's not about who she *really* is, but who she projects. I'm going to get a purple streak!"

"To project what, precisely?"

Bam! The door rattled on its hinges as two young children burst into the garage/laundry room/salon.

"Mama, we're bored."

"Mama, we want another snack!"

The woman grabbed a little hand by the wrist. "Get back, you'll smear cracker on me. Didn't I tell you to stay in the car?"

The little girl's lower lip trembled.

"We want candy!" her brother shouted.

"Get in the car!" their mother shouted. She threw her phone into her purse and stood. "Your lateness has cost you a client." She stomped out the door.

The woman getting the perm and Myrtle eyed each other. Myrtle shrugged and continued wrapping.

"Well, shame on me," Annabelle said.

"What do you mean, Sister?"

"I wanted to be like that woman simply because she was pretty. And she's a woman who yells at her children for not wanting to sit in a stuffy car!"

"Well, their hands were quite sticky."

"Still, ugly is as ugly does."

"That sounds like something I would say," Lillybelle said. "Not my free-spirited sister."

"Well, *you* weren't caught up by her appearance, were you?"

"Annabelle, I can start you now," Myrtle said.

Still frowning, Annabelle settled herself in the chair.

"The usual?" Myrtle asked.

"Yes."

Lillybelle spoke up, "Not the usual. She wants a purple streak."

Annabelle stared at her sister in surprise. "You want me to look like that ugly woman?"

"No, I want you to look like what you are. A woman of mystery who *could* be on her way to a clandestine rendezvous, but instead chooses to go sort clothes for the church clothing giveaway."

"Why, Sister," Annabelle said, "you say the nicest things." She settled back in the chair, a smile covering her face. "One purple streak, Myrtle. And make it pop!"

A Thought. . . Our thoughts, words and actions make our lives pretty. After all, we don't want to hear our mothers' voice in our head saying, "Don't act ugly," do we? ~Mischelle Creager

A Scripture. . . Stop judging by mere appearances, but instead judge correctly. John 7:24

And a Prayer. . . Dear Father, forgive me when I judge someone by their appearance. Help me to look where you do – on the inside. In Jesus' name, Amen

Always walk in line,
Remember "please" and "thank you"
Important knowledge

CHAPTER SEVEN

Coaching Little League

Annabelle slipped her cell phone back into her jeans' pocket. "That was Coach Bill. Megan went into labor. They're on their way to the hospital."

Lillybelle eyed the little boys running in and around the dusty dugout. "Does that mean we forfeit?"

"Don't be silly. He has two perfectly good assistant coaches to take over for him."

"Who?"

"Us." Annabelle clapped her hands. "Settle down, boys! The game is about to start."

Lillybelle protested. "We don't know anything about baseball. We simply offered to help Bill because there was no one else to do it."

"And now he needs help. And here we are! Batter up!"

Amid the cheers and whistles of his teammates, little William grabbed a bat and ran to the mound.

Strike one! Strike two! Strike three!

"Oh, dear. William is out," Annabelle said. "Sister, look how he's slumping."

"Such a defeated look," Lillybelle agreed. She called, "Stand up straight, dear."

"William!" a voice from the crowd yelled. "What kind of swing was that? I told you to keep your eye on the ball!"

Little William's shoulders drooped even further. His tennis shoes kicked up puffs of dirt as he shuffled back to the dugout.

"Who's shrieking?" Annabelle asked.

Lillybelle squinted toward the chain link fence. "I believe it's William's mother. She seems rather upset."

"Over a missed ball? I'd be more worried about his posture. You don't get anywhere in life with defeated posture."

"Agreed, Sister."

Soon William came up to bat again.

"Oh, my," Annabelle muttered. "This just isn't his day, is it?"

"William, are you blind?" his mother bellowed over the noisy crowd. "After the game, it's batting cages instead of ice cream."

William's shoulders slumped. He kicked the base before leaving it.

"Let me see that nice straight posture next time you go out," Annabelle told him as he plopped on the dugout bench.

"I'm a loser," he replied.

"Not with good posture, you're not. As your coach, I want to see it next time you bat." She turned and whispered to Lillybelle, "We've got to do something."

"Agreed," Lillybelle said.

At the beginning of the fourth inning, the sisters strolled over to the fence. They stood to the left and right of William's mother.

"Have you ever thought about calling bingo?" Lillybelle asked her.

The woman frowned. "Why, er, no."

"You should. You have such a loud, firm voice."

"We're worried about William," Annabelle told her.

"Oh I know it," the woman said. "He can't hit worth anything today. I..."

"His posture," Annabelle interrupted gently.

"I'm sorry? His posture?"

"He has the posture of a child who's given up. We don't want dear William to give up, do we?"

"Um, no. I guess not."

William came up to bat.

Swing. And a miss.

Swing. And a miss.

Another swing and, "OUT!" shouted the umpire.

William drew his foot back to kick the base again. But when he caught sight of the sisters, he slowly straightened his shoulders.

"Way to go, William," Lillybelle yelled. "That's the type of posture we like to see."

"Yes, way to go," Annabelle agreed. She gave him a thumbs up.

The sisters turned to his mother.

"Um, good posture, William," she called. "You, er, look like a winner."

The frown on William's face lightened. He stood even straighter as he ran toward the dugout.

"Way to go, Mom," Annabelle said. She patted the woman's arm.

"Stevie, why didn't you swing at that ball? Quit daydreaming!" a man down the fence screamed.

"Oh dear," Lillybelle said. "You'll have to excuse us. We've got to go coach Mr. Davis now."

A Thought... Words are powerful. They can help or hurt, build up and break down, cripple or heal. Used carelessly, they can damage a heart or mind beyond repair. Used correctly, they can lead someone to great heights. ~ Mischelle Creager

A Scripture... *"May these words of my mouth and this meditation of my heart be pleasing in your sight, Lord, my Rock and my Redeemer."* ~ Psalm 19:14

A Prayer... Dear Lord, may my words always reflect You. Give me the wisdom to stop and think before I speak so that I don't hurt others or hinder You. In Jesus' name, Amen

Personality
One per individual
Can't borrow or trade

CHAPTER EIGHT

Flighty vs. Stubborn

"Why aren't you getting ready?" Lillybelle inquired. Annabelle looked up from where she sat working a crossword puzzle. "All I have to do is slip on my shoes."

"Which will probably take you ten minutes to find." Lillybelle washed out her tea cup and folded an embroidered dishcloth neatly on the kitchen counter. "The movie starts in thirty minutes, and it's a twenty minute drive to the theater."

"Which gives us a half hour of wiggle room."

"Didn't you hear me? The movie starts at 1:00."

Annabelle shook her head. "No, Sister, it starts at 1:30."

Hands on hips, Lillybelle glared. "Annabelle Verline Kingston, you have to be the *most* flighty person I've ever met. The movie starts at 1:00. Where are your shoes?"

"They're beside the back door. Sister, the movie doesn't start until 1:30. Look it up if you don't believe me."

"I don't need to look it up."

Annabelle sighed. "That's you all over, Lillybelle Maudine Granger. Stubborn! I sure hope when our Savior comes back you don't argue with him about where Heaven is located."

"I have no reason to think He's as flighty as you are, dear. He knows the way. Now come on. You know I hate walking in late to a movie."

Annabelle rolled her eyes, put aside her crossword puzzle and went to get her shoes. She found Primrose lying in the left one. Annabelle scratched the purring cat behind the ears. "I'll bet you'd like some Kitty Kibble."

"Oh dear," sighed Lillybelle.

"Now, Sister, you get fed when you're hungry."

"Humph," replied Lillybelle.

Primrose taken care of, they headed for the movie theater. As she drove, Annabelle glanced sideways at her sister. "I do hope you won't be too stubborn to apologize when you find out you're wrong."

Lillybelle sniffed. "And maybe you'll learn a lesson about being flighty when you see that I'm right."

Twenty minutes later they pulled into the parking lot of the Grand Theater. "See, no one else is going in," Annabelle said. "We're too early."

"Hmmm...."

A minute later, they stood in front of the box office.

Annabelle shook her head. "It started at noon. I guess I do need to be less flighty."

"Well, it does come in handy sometimes," Lillybelle said. "I mean, if you weren't so flighty, we wouldn't have taken that wrong turn last week and stumbled upon that pretty little pond. It will be so nice have a picnic beside it this summer. It's my fault. I shouldn't have been so stubborn."

"Your stubbornness has kept us from doing some foolish things. You know, flighty and stubborn aren't a bad combination - except when it comes to movie times."

"Well said. Come on, Flighty. We may have missed out on the popcorn, but there's an ice cream parlor just down the block."

"Lead the way, Stubborn, lead the way."

A Thought. . . Tolerate and celebrate differences. After all, I'm sure your friends and family are overlooking the fact that you aren't *quite* perfect either.

A Scripture. . . *"As it is, there are many parts, but one body."* ~Ecclesiastes 3:1

And a Prayer. . . Dear Father, you made me unique, and you made everyone else unique also. I need to remember people don't have to be exactly like me. You love variety. You created it! In Jesus' name, Amen

Rejoice and be glad
For you are a soul the Lord
Has made beautiful

CHAPTER NINE

Say "Cheese"

Lillybelle leaned back in the porch swing and turned the page of the album resting in her lap. "Do you remember this one?"

Annabelle reached out and swished a blade of grass off the photo. "That was at Uncle Fred's, the year Cousin Emma Sue had to... you know."

"Have a shotgun wedding?"

"Now, Sister, the baby was a preemie."

Lillybelle snorted. "No eight pound baby is a preemie." She studied the photograph. "Daddy looks so handsome with his mustache. Look! Is that ketchup on your dress?"

"It was. From a food fight with Cousin Luke." Annabelle indicated the next photo. "This was taken at the beach."

"Obviously. Daddy's pretending to throw you into the ocean."

"And you're pouting because you're afraid he's going to splash you and get your swimsuit wet."

Lillybelle patted her wavy gray hair. "I've always felt it important to act like a lady."

Annabelle ignored the remark. Instead, she leaned back in the porch swing, a thoughtful look on her face. "Sister, have you noticed there are very few pictures of Mother?"

Lillybelle nodded. "She didn't like having her picture taken."

"True. She always said she needed to get her hair done or put on nicer clothes or lose weight." Annabelle reached out and gently touched the picture of her father holding her high over the waves. "I love looking at these pictures of Daddy."

"So do I. It makes me wish we had more of Mother, though."

Annabelle grinned. "I have a great idea. Wait here." The screen door banged shut and in a moment she was back with the camera.

"Oh dear, Sister. What do you have in mind?" Lillybelle asked.

"Your Michael asked for a picture, didn't he?"

"And I intend to send him one as soon as I get my hair done. I'm going to make an appointment..."

"You sound just like Mother! Do you really think that's the kind of picture he wants? When we look at these pictures, which ones do we love? Certainly not the posed ones."

"But..."

"Here comes Mr. Daughterly. He'll take a picture of us." Annabelle waved to the mailman. "Yoo hoo!"

"Hello, ladies, what can I do for you?"

"Would you take a picture of us?" Annabelle inquired.

"Why sure." He set his mailbag on the ground and took the camera.

Lillybelle started to her feet. "Let me just brush--"

"You stay right there," Annabelle ordered. "Now, smile and wave. Oh wait. Here kitty, kitty." She reached down and scooped up Primrose. Primrose, who had been dozing at Annabelle's feet, meowed a slight protest. "It won't hurt you to pose for the camera," Annabelle told her. "We're ready," she instructed Mr. Daughterly.

CLICK

"Here you go," the mailman said, giving the camera back to Annabelle.

"Thank you," Annabelle said.

"No problem." He waved and went on his way.

"Now, Sister," Annabelle said, "let's see how it turned out."

Both sisters held their heads close and peered at the small screen. Two old ladies smiled from the porch swing. The wind whipped their hair as they waved. In Annabelle's lap sat a grumpy looking cat.

"I need to lose weight," Lillybelle said.

Annabelle laughed. "Michael won't see that, Sister. He'll just see his mother and his favorite aunt --"

"--his only aunt."

"--sitting on their front porch in front of the house he grew up in. He'll love it."

"Yes, I suppose he will."

A Thought. . . Don't worry about pictures being photo perfect. Life isn't perfect, and neither are the best memories.

A Scripture. . . *"Charm is deceitful, and beauty is vain, but a woman who fears the Lord is to be praised."* Proverbs 31:30

And a Prayer... Father, please don't let me get so caught up in appearance that I forget to enjoy this life you've given me. I need to focus on the inside, the spiritual side, to be the most beautiful person I can be. In Jesus' name, Amen

A river's branches
Flowing apart, now entwined
Two halves of a soul

CHAPTER TEN

Playing Matchmaker

"Look! Look!" Annabelle ordered. "Sister, are you looking?"

Lillybelle frowned. "Calm yourself. The only excuse for that much excitement is spotting the Lord himself returning. Have these park benches always been this hard?"

"Oh, pshaw." Annabelle waved a hand as if swatting away Lillybelle's remark. "Do you see them?"

Lillybelle peered over her glasses. "Why, it's Crystal Evans. By the looks of those purple sweats, I'd say she's about to go jogging. Sister, haven't you seen anyone jog before?"

"Oh, hush. You know how we're always saying Crystal needs to meet a nice man?"

"Yes, I do." Lillybelle studied the people milling around them. "Are you thinking about the man in the tank top that says "No fat chicks" or the one who just spilled his sno-cone? Personally, I think the tank top gentleman needs to take a good look in the -- "

"--No, over there!"

Lillybelle gazed in the new direction. "Isn't that the new youth intern getting coffee from Lots-a-Latte? What's his name?"

"Jack... Jake... Jackson!" Annabelle said.

"That's it, Jackson," Lillybelle agreed.

"Wouldn't they make the cutest couple?"

"Yes, they would!" Then Lillybelle frowned. "But you know how young people are. They'd rather meet a stranger over the internet than be set up. Especially by two--"

"--old busybodies?"

Lillybelle huffed. "I was going to say experienced matchmakers."

Annabelle frowned. "The trick is to make sure they don't know it's a setup. I just know if they meet, it'll be love at first sight."

"What have you got in mind?"

"Let's try 'The Old Lady in Distress.'" Annabelle pulled out a handful of change from her polka dotted change purse and tossed it to the ground. "Oh, dear," she cried. "I don't know if my arthritic fingers can pick up all these small coins."

"I do know you can't act," Lillybelle whispered.

"Hush."

Crystal hurried over. "Miss Kingston, is that you? Let me help."

"Thank you," Annabelle gushed. She looked sideways at Lillybelle, who shook her head.

"Here you go," Crystal said with a grin.

Annabelle opened her coin purse. "Thank you, Crystal. You are so nice to help. And you did it so fast."

"Anytime." The young woman jumped to her feet, strolled over to the jogging path and resumed her stretching.

"What happened to Jackson?" Annabelle inquired.

"He's on the phone," Lillybelle informed her. "Probably talking to a dating service as we speak. Any more bright ideas?"

"Yes. Hide my phone," Annabelle ordered.

"What?"

Annabelle shoved her phone into Lillybelle's hands and closed her eyes tightly.

"What are you doing?" Lillybelle demanded.

"Making sure I don't tell a lie. Is it hidden?"

Lillybelle sighed and slipped the phone into Annabelle's purse. "Yes."

Annabelle opened her eyes. "Oh, dear, oh dear, I can't find it anywhere!" She clapped her hands to her face and moaned.

"We really must get you acting lessons," her sister muttered.

Annabelle ignored her. "Oh, what am I going to do?"

Jackson hurried over. "What can I... hey, don't I know you from church?"

"Yes." Annabelle beamed. "I'm Annabelle Kingston and this is my sister Lillybelle Granger. You're the new youth intern, right?"

He grinned. "Jackson Davis. Can I help you with something?"

Annabelle smiled. "Well, I seem to have misplaced my phone. You know how old people are, always losing things."

"Young people too," he replied with a laugh. "Let me help you look."

Jackson put down his coffee and searched under the bench. Annabelle searched on top of it. She glanced over at Lillybelle who shook her head and pointed to her ears.

Annabelle peered toward Crystal who showed signs of finishing her warm up. Two cords hung from the young woman's ears. Earbuds.

"I'm sorry, Ms. Kingston, but I can't seem to find your phone anywhere," Jackson said as he stood. "Are you sure you brought it with you?"

"Why, look, Sister. Here it is in your purse," Lillybelle said sweetly. She smiled at the youth intern. "Old people can be so forgetful."

"Well, I'm glad you found it. See you in church." He headed in the opposite direction from where Crystal jogged in place.

"Well, pooh," Annabelle said. "That idea clearly didn't work. We'll have to..."

"Go home," Lillybelle declared. "If those two young people are to meet today, then God Almighty Himself will have to plan it." She stood, took a step and immediately fell down.

"Sister!" Annabelle cried. She knelt beside the prone Lillybelle.

"My foot slipped," Lillybelle moaned.

Crystal knelt on her other side. ""Miss Granger? Are you okay?"

"What happened?" Jackson asked, peering anxiously over Annabelle's shoulder.

Lillybelle moaned again. "My foot slipped."

Crystal reached out and picked up a quarter. "Uh, oh. I think it's my fault. I didn't get all the change."

Lillybelle glared at Annabelle. "Oh, I don't think it's *your* fault."

"Oh, Sister, I'm so sorry."

Jackson shook his head. "You can never be too careful. I think we'd better take you to the hospital. Let me pull my car around."

"But our van is here," Annabelle protested. "By the way, Jackson, this is Crystal. Crystal, Jackson is the new youth intern at church."

Lillybelle rolled her eyes, whether in pain or in annoyance, Annabelle wasn't sure.

Crystal smiled. "Why don't I drive your van to the hospital, and then Jackson can drive me back here to get my car?"

"That sounds like a lovely idea," Annabelle said. "In fact, why don't we wait here while you go with him to get his car?"

Jackson lifted Lillybelle onto the bench. Then he and Crystal hurried away.

"I can't believe you slipped on a coin," Annabelle exclaimed.

Lillybelle smiled. "Pretty good acting, huh?"

Annabelle stared. "Sister, you lied?"

"Nope, I improvised. The good Lord did the rest."

"What do you mean?"

Lillybelle grimaced. "I really did twist my ankle. Look, it's starting to swell."

"Well," Annabelle observed, "it's a good thing we're already taking you to the hospital. Do you think God had a hand in this?"

"Of course," Lillybelle replied. "Even God needs a good belly laugh now and then."

A thought. . . We can't always see God's plan working and that can be scary. Faith takes a lot of courage. But there is power in belief. And there is comfort in knowing God is in charge and He never fails or forsakes.

A scripture. . . *"For I know the plans I have for you," declares the Lord, "plans to prosper you and not to harm you, plans to give you hope and a future."* Jeremiah 29:11

And a prayer. . . Dear Father, I know your way is best. Help me when I can't see the path you put before me. Help me to trust in you to help me find my way until your son comes again. In Jesus' name, Amen

Surging emotion
A churning, rushing river
Cascading torrent

CHAPTER ELEVEN

A Basketful of Pride

"Sister, I believe we planted too much zucchini," Annabelle observed. She brushed the dirt off the knees of her jeans.

Lillybelle stood and stretched. "I told you more than one grows to a vine."

"Yes, Sister, you did." Annabelle studied the vegetable garden. "The tomatoes are having a good year."

"As are the green beans. If you'd like, we can take some to the food pantry."

"Actually, I've another idea. You know that dear Mr. Waynesboro? He lost his job."

Lillybelle nodded. "With two children, that has to be hard."

"Well, instead of the food pantry, why don't we take a basket of vegetables to the Waynesboroes? The children might not appreciate it, but the parents will."

"That sounds wonderful, Sister. That green basket, the one Michael gave me filled with bath soaps, would be perfect."

"Whatever happened to those soaps?" Annabelle asked.

"I re-gifted them. That boy knows I don't like lavender."

"It's the thought that counts," Annabelle murmured.

"Well, for it to count, there should be a thought and not a half price sale tag," her sister replied.

"This is fun," Annabelle remarked as they assembled the veggie basket. "You know, Sister. I think we should make it a surprise. Let's sneak the basket onto the porch."

"Seems easier just to ring the doorbell and say 'here,' but if that's what you want to do, I won't argue." Lillybelle tied a big yellow ribbon around the handle. "There. Done."

"Isn't this exciting?" Annabelle whispered walking across the lawn.

"You need to get out more," Lillybelle replied.

After a moment's fussing, Lillybelle dragged her sister away from the porch. "It's not a surprise if they open the door and see your rear end sticking up over the basket."

Back home, they'd barely cleaned the kitchen when the doorbell rang.

Annabelle opened the door. Mr. Waynesboro stood on the porch holding their basket.

"Why, hello," she said.

"Does this belong to you?"

Annabelle frowned. "Well, I guess, technically the basket was ours, but..."

"I mean the food inside the basket."

Lillybelle joined Annabelle at the door. "Hello, Christopher."

"Hello." He glared at Annabelle. "Does it?"

"Well, yes, the vegetables came from our garden. The Lord provided us with a bounty this year and..."

"And you thought you'd pass on some charity to the man who can't take care of his family."

Annabelle's mouth dropped open.

"We were sharing," Lillybelle explained.

"That's not what I call it." He set the basket on their porch. "I call it charity. I can take care of my family, ladies." With that he stomped off down the wood steps and headed for home.

"Well, I'll be," Annabelle stated.

"Didn't see that coming," Lillybelle said. "The stubborn fool."

"I never thought of it as charity," Annabelle said. She picked up the basket. "Just being neighborly."

Lillybelle patted her on the back. "I know, Sister, I know."

That afternoon, an unusually quiet Annabelle stared out the front window, a frown covering her face.

Lillybelle put down her crochet. "I'm in the mood for cupcakes."

"I don't feel like baking," Annabelle said.

"Who said anything about baking? Let's go to Angels and Roses Tearoom."

Annabelle brightened. "Why, Sister, that's a lovely idea."

Outside, Annabelle tried the key in the van. "Rrr. . . rrr. . . rrr," was the discouraging noise she heard from the starter.

"Start it, Sister," Lillybelle suggested.

"I'm trying, but it's not cooperating."

Knock , knock.

"Eeek," Annabelle shrieked.

Lillybelle leaned around her. "Mercy! Roll the window down, and say hello to Mr. Waynesboro."

"Can I help?" their neighbor asked.

"It won't start," Annabelle replied.

"Well, let's..."

"No, thank you," Lillybelle said.

Both Annabelle and Mr. Waynesboro stared at her.

"We don't accept charity," Lillybelle said.

"Charity? It's not..."

Annabelle winked at her sister then sighed loudly. "I guess we're going to have to live right here in this van for the rest of our lives."

"Why, that's silly," he insisted.

"Isn't it though," Lillybelle said.

Mr. Waynesboro chuckled. "Okay, ladies, I get it. Let's say after I help you with your van, I pick up that basket of vegetables."

Annabelle beamed. "Sounds like a good plan."

"I'll get my tools."

"Pride goeth before a fall," Lillybelle quoted as he walked away. Mr. Waynesboro tripped. "Well, now. That was just timing."

A Thought... My grandmother used to say, "Don't deny me the opportunity to serve God by serving you." Don't let pride keep *you* from experiencing the full love of the Christian family God has given you.

A Scripture... "Pride goes before destruction, a haughty spirit before a fall." Proverbs 16:18

And a Prayer... Dear Father, pride gets me into so much trouble. Especially when I refuse to ask for help when I need it. You made me to look after others, Father. And, you made others to look after me. Help me to remember that. In Jesus' name, Amen

As the warm sun shines
Eyes close and muscles weaken
Melting energy

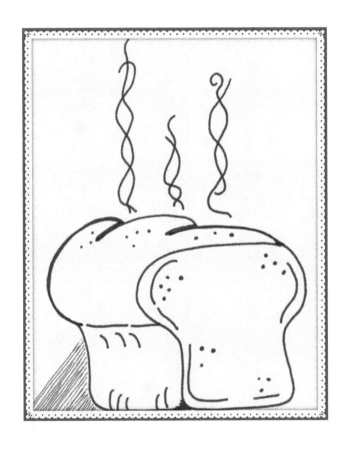

CHAPTER TWELVE

Getting Some Help

"The jungles of Africa," Annabelle said. "The deep, dark woods."

Lillybelle adjusted her glasses as she peered over her crochet. "I beg your pardon?"

Annabelle tapped on the bay window. "I'm naming things our front yard is starting to resemble."

Lillybelle sniffed. "Doesn't sound very productive to me. Why don't you come help me crochet caps for the preemies at the hospital?" She bent to disentangle Primrose from her red yarn.

Thwarted, the cat yawned and strolled away to show she wasn't really interested in playing anyway.

Annabelle shook her head. "You know I always lose count, and my caps turn out lopsided. Sister, we really need to do something about our lawn."

Lillybelle sighed. Putting down her yarn, she joined Annabelle at the window. "Do you know how to wield a machete?"

Annabelle's look turned blissful. "It might be fun to learn."

"You can't work the lawn mower, but you think you can swing a machete?"

"I know perfectly well how to work a lawnmower." Annabelle rubbed the back of one hand. "It's just a little much for my arthritis."

Lillybelle patted Annabelle on the arm. "I know, Sister, I know. As I've watched you get old..."

"You're two years older than I am!"

"Even so, we've got to do something about that lawn. Maybe we could call the church and get on the list for a youth service project?"

"That's an idea," Annabelle said. "Although, I'm sure there are others who could use the help more than we can."

"Then what have you got in mind?"

"Remember when Mr. Waynesboro confused our neighborly offer of fresh vegetables with charity?"

Lillybelle shook her head over the silliness of some people. "Yes, I do!"

"Well, maybe that's our problem?"

"Being proud?"

"Being too proud to ask for help."

"You're right. You know, Mr. Waynesboro did a great job getting our van started that day. Maybe he could help with our grass."

"I have a better idea. Follow me." Annabelle led the way into the craft room. "I know we have some poster board in here somewhere."

"It's in the cabinet where it belongs. Sister, what are you up to?"

Annabelle laid the poster board on the white, shabby chic craft table. "Hand me that purple marker, please."

Lillybelle watched for a moment then smiled. "Why, Sister, I think this is an excellent idea."

A few moments later, a sign was taped to their flower stenciled mailbox.

Needed:

Someone to cut grass

In trade:

Fresh baked bread

"Let's see what happens," Annabelle said.

A half-hour later, Josh Ledbetter rang their doorbell. "Hello, Mrs. Kingston. Has anybody claimed that bread yet?"

"Why no, Josh."

"I'll mow your lawn."

"That sounds fine, Josh. The lawnmower is in the shed. The bread will be waiting for you when you finish." Annabelle shut the door and rushed to tell Lillybelle, "It worked! Josh is going to cut our grass."

"Perfect. You know, his mama is a single mother with two growing boys to feed. We should throw in some homemade jam."

"And maybe some of my ginger cookies," Annabelle mused.

"I have one of my famous tuna casseroles in the freezer."

"If we add a gallon of sun tea, they'll have dinner for tonight."

Lillybelle smiled. "A very cheap price to pay for getting that lawn mowed."

"It surely is, Sister."

A Thought... A little bit of thought and time can make a big difference in someone else's life.

A Scripture... "Carry each other's burdens, and in this way you will fulfill the law of Christ." Galatians 6:2

And a Prayer... Dear Father, selfishness and yes, laziness, often keep me from helping. Forgive me and help me to work on having a more loving heart. In Jesus' name, Amen

Burdens so weary
I lift up my soul and pray
Jesus takes my pain

CHAPTER THIRTEEN

Forgiving Yourself

Annabelle sat on the porch steps, shoulders slumping. "I can't believe I ruined the whole surprise."

Lillybelle joined her on the step. "You didn't mean to. Although Frank did spend the entire last month planning his wife's seventieth birthday party."

Annabelle buried her head in her hands. "I thought I took Carrie off the list. I didn't mean to send her the e-vite."

"Frank knows that. He even joked about not having the strain of keeping a secret from Carrie, his first in fifty-two years of marriage."

"He's sweet. But I really screwed up this time."

"Carrie isn't mad. In fact, didn't she check the 'attending' box on her e-vite?"

"Yes, she's a good sport."

"Frank's forgiven you. Carrie's forgiven you. There's only one person left."

Annabelle straightened. She pushed her shoulders back. "Okay, okay, I forgive myself."

"Good girl. But you know what the most ironic thing is?"

"What?

"You're supposed to be the computer whiz!"

A Thought... Jesus said in Luke 6:31 - "Do to others as you would have them do to you." If someone offends you, especially if they don't mean to, and they apologize, don't you forgive them and go on? You give them forgiveness and let them go in peace. Why not let them do the same for you? Accept their forgiveness and go in peace. ~Mischelle Creager

A Scripture... *"For I will forgive their wickedness and will remember their sins no more."* Hebrews 8:12

And a prayer... Dear God, everyone makes mistakes. Your word tells me to forgive, or I can't be forgiven. Help me realize that also means forgiving *myself* as I forgive others. In Jesus' name, Amen

Time marches on ~we're
Older and misunderstood
Seems we matter none

~ Robin Miley Totten

CHAPTER FOURTEEN

Taking On the Box Boy

Young Jonathan loaded Lillybelle's groceries into the van. "Mom said you've been sick."

Lillybelle considered it in ill taste to discuss one's health. Especially with someone sporting metal objects thrust through his tongue. But Jonathan's mother, Sarah, led the Tuesday morning Ladies' Bible class, so Lillybelle strove to be cordial. "I've just recovered from a little cold."

"Well, at your age, you can't be too careful."

Lillybelle lifted a manicured eyebrow. "Do tell."

Jonathan stuffed a bag in the van a little harder than Lillybelle liked and grinned. "Well, you know, it's not like heaven's that far away."

"I beg your pardon?"

"Of course," he continued, as her eggs took an adventure on top of the bread, "I guess it gets easier."

"Easier?"

"When you get old." He grinned again. "What have you got left to live for?"

Lillybelle drew herself up straight. "Life, young man, I have life to live for."

§

Back home in her cozy kitchen, Lillybelle plopped a nylon tote bag on the yellow Formica table. "Annabelle."

Annabelle lifted the eggs off the bread and placed them in the refrigerator. "Yes?"

"I have a new goal in life."

"And what is that?"

"To outlive the box boy at Applewood's Market and Deli."

Annabelle frowned. "Sarah's boy?"

"Yes."

"You intend to outlive a seventeen year old?"

Lillybelle folded her arms and stood a little straighter. "He called me old and implied I had nothing to live for. I'll show him."

Annabelle laughed. "Yes, Sister, I have no doubt you will."

A Thought... Whether it is creating and keeping a beautiful garden, going to all fifty state capitals, or baking cupcakes for the neighborhood kids, enjoy the time God has given you. Treasure each day. ~ Mischelle Creager

A Scripture... *"Gray hair is a crown of splendor; it is attained in the way of righteousness."* Proverbs 16:31

A prayer... Lord, too many times I allow others to stifle my desires, even for your word. Give me courage to make my own choices. My life can glorify You, no matter what my age. In Jesus' name, Amen

Perfection defined
God made the sound of laughter
On a child's lips

CHAPTER FIFTEEN

Taking Time for Themselves. . .Sort Of

"That Chelsea Waynesboro just goes and goes," Annabelle remarked as she gazed out the front window. She bent backward in a superb yoga stretch.

"Young people these days don't know how to relax," Lillybelle replied. She settled into her easy chair, Primrose on her lap. "Some days all I need are my slippers and my crochet."

"Of course," Annabelle reflected as she bent forward, "if I had two little tots, I might be a little less inclined to put my feet up."

"Are you suggesting I'm lazy?"

"No, Sister dear, I'm simply saying that we have plenty of time for pampering ourselves."

Lillybelle sighed. "You're right, of course. Maybe we need to re-think our 'me' time."

"Exactly what I was thinking," Annabelle replied.

§

"Have you ever baked ginger cookies before?" Annabelle asked Charlotte. The sisters' worn Formica table was covered with baking supplies.

The curly-haired moppet shook her head.

"You have flour on your nose," Carly told her sister with a giggle.

Charlotte frowned and her rosebud lips puckered.

Annabelle dipped her finger in the flour. "Well then, she'd better share, right?" She touched her own nose and then Carly's. Both girls giggled. "Sister?" Annabelle called. "You're missing out on the fun."

Lillybelle turned from the window overlooking the breakfast nook. "I don't think Chelsea has left yet."

"She's not leaving," Carly said. She splatted a piece of dough flat. The next piece she popped into her mouth.

Lillybelle frowned. "But this is supposed to be your mother's 'me' time."

"Mama's taking a nap," Charlotte said. "And Carly's sneaking cookies!"

Annabelle laughed. "A nap is probably the best 'me' time a young mother can take." She picked up a piece of cookie dough and worked it until it was nice and round. Then she tilted her head back. The girls watched in awe as she tossed the dough high in the air and caught it in her mouth. "Yum!"

Fresh giggles and enthusiastic hand claps.

"You'd think there were three children making cookies," Lillybelle said. "But I do believe you are right, Sister." She joined them at the kitchen table. "I suggest we take this type of 'me' time for ourselves at least once a week." She grinned. "Now, let me show you how to really cannonball cookie dough!"

A Thought... Even in old age we can help and share with others. It doesn't have to be something big. A plate of cookies, a note of encouragement to someone struggling, a few words of appreciation for a mother overwhelmed with raising her children (maybe along with that plate of cookies) can be all it takes to brighten someone's day. And, oh, the joy it will also bring to the giver. ~ Mischelle Creager

A Scripture... *"Not looking to your own interests but each of you to the interests of the others.* ~ Philippians 2:4

And a Prayer... Dear God, please help me to remember that sometimes the best "me" time occurs when helping others. In Jesus' name, Amen

Sweet, sweet solitude
Unbearable loneliness
A flip of the coin

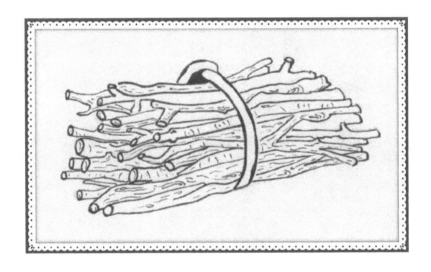

CHAPTER SIXTEEN

Taking a Timeout

Annabelle closed the door to the daycare's two-year-old room. "Wasn't that fun, Sister?"

Lillybelle brushed at her denim skirt. "I think I sat in something sticky."

"The daycare reading program is just wonderful," Annabelle continued as they walked to their van. "The kids really enjoyed us reading to them."

"All but that one little stinker." Lillybelle settled in the passenger side seat of the van and rummaged in her purse for a Kleenex. "Do you think it's candy?"

Annabelle started the van. "Do I think what's candy?"

"This sticky spot on my skirt."

"I don't believe the daycare gives them candy. Maybe it's apple juice."

Lillybelle gave up on the spot. "That one little boy didn't enjoy us reading to him at all."

"He seemed tired, Sister. You know as well as I do, it doesn't take much to overwhelm a two-year-old."

"Well, I certainly think he deserved that timeout after the fit he threw."

"Timeout isn't a punishment," Annabelle explained. "It's a time for the little ones to get control. At least that's how the aide explained it to me while you were reading. Sometimes little ones need a place to calm down."

Lillybelle peered up at the sky. "Humph, looks like rain."

Fat drops hit the windshield as Annabelle pulled the van into the garage. "Looks like a big storm. I'm glad we'll be snug inside." Once inside their cozy kitchen, she set about brewing a pot of ginger tea.

The storm lingered into the evening.

"It would be nice to have a fire," Lillybelle remarked.

"It's too bad neither of us thought to bring in some wood."

"You're always on that computer. Why didn't you check the forecast?"

"I believe they still show the forecast on something called the TV," Annabelle replied. "Why didn't *you* check it?"

Lillybelle pulled her shawl closer around her shoulders. "It's cold. Even Primrose wishes there was a fire."

The cat blinked from her bed in front of the fireplace then promptly went back to sleep.

"We could turn up the heat," Annabelle suggested.

"Too expensive. *And* a complete waste, since we have plenty of wood for a nice, warm fire," Lillybelle protested.

The wind shook the house as rain splattered the picture window. "I'm not going out in that, even to the back porch," Annabelle declared.

"You know I have bad knees," Lillybelle replied. "Do you want me to fall and break my neck on the stairs?"

"Yes, of course, Sister. That's exactly what I want."

"Was that sarcasm?"

Annabelle stood up.

"Where are you going?" Lillybelle asked.

"I'm giving myself a timeout. When I'm sure I'm not in danger of hitting you over the head with the broom, I'll come back down."

"Sarcasm again?"

"No."

"Have a nice timeout."

"Thank you, Sister."

A Thought... Unfortunately, we don't always have the luxury of finding a quiet corner. But we can take a deep breath and think before we speak. How much pain and hurt could be avoided if we took a little mental timeout before speaking our minds?

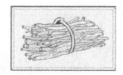

A Scripture... *"Set a guard, O LORD, over my mouth; Keep watch over the door of my lips."* Psalms 141:3

And a Prayer... Oh, Lord, does my mouth get me into trouble! I need to think before I speak and give myself a "timeout," so that when I do speak, my words come from Your wisdom and Your will. In Jesus' name, Amen

Fairies in wagons
Unicorns amid dragons
Imagination

CHAPTER SEVENTEEN

Just Imagine

"I love touring these old houses," Annabelle said.

"My feet hurt," Lillybelle replied.

"Everyone stay on the sidewalk," the tour group leader called from up ahead. "You're in for a treat. This is one of the oldest houses in our fair town. It's definitely a 'grand dame'."

"You think they'd take the time to weed a 'grand dame,'" Lillybelle said.

"Shhh," Annabelle said.

The tour guide continued, "The owners are having some work done, so the antique doorknocker that usually hangs on the front door is missing. Just imagine a stately brass lion head. Of course, they also plan to paint, so you'll also have to imagine the door without chips."

"How much did we pay for this tour?" Lillybelle whispered.

"Shhh," Annabelle said.

The front door flew open and their hostess stood in the entrance. She wore a flowing orange caftan and on her head perched a blazing pink flowered turban.

"Oh my," Lillybelle said.

"Sh… you're right," Annabelle said.

"Welcome to the Grand Duchess, as we like to call our home," the owner boomed. "Can everyone hear me?"

Everyone agreed they could hear just fine.

"Well then," the woman said. She turned and swooshed into the house.

After a confused moment, the group followed.

"Oh...," Lillybelle started.

"....my," Annabelle finished.

"Now," the owner said, "I'm sure you've noticed our Duchess needs a little work. We're in the process of completely restoring her. The historical society asked if we wanted to take her off the tour, but we didn't want anyone to miss seeing the Duchess. We'll just have to use our imaginations."

"Pardon me?" Lillybelle whispered.

"We're supposed to keep an open mind," Annabelle explained.

The group paused in front of a hulking hole in the wall. Scattered lumber and burnt ashes littered the floor.

"This was once a walk-in fireplace," the owner informed them. "And it will be again. Just imagine stone reaching from floor to ceiling. This fireplace, when finished, will be able to heat the entire downstairs."

Peering into the exposed hole, Lillybelle wrinkled her nose. "At the moment, all I can imagine are the mice that must live in that mess."

"Did you say you saw a mouse?" a woman in a pale blue pantsuit inquired in horror.

"There are no mice in the Grand Duchess," the owner stated. She gave Lillybelle a withering look. "Now, here is where the pride of the Duchess will stand. Just imagine a circular staircase winding its way to the second floor. Wrought iron with marble spindles." She clasped her hands to her chest. "It will be breathtaking, I can assure you. Now, let me show you what we have planned for the pantry."

"You know," Annabelle whispered. "It's kind of like imagining what heaven will be like." She waved a hand. "Imagine, the pearly gates swinging out in front of you."

Lillybelle chuckled. She also waved a hand. "Streets of gold leading to beautiful mansions."

The sisters realized a silence had fallen around them. The owner glared at them, her turban slightly askew.

"We're very sorry," Lillybelle said.

"We were just imagining," Annabelle said innocently.

"Yes, well," the woman huffed, "as I was saying, just imagine..."

"I believe lunch is next on the tour," Annabelle whispered.

"As long as we don't have to imagine it," Lillybelle replied.

A Thought... Every morning we get up with the opportunity to create our world. Do you look at the negative or the positive? Is your sense of humor drained? We make the choice to be angry, impatient and sarcastic. Today, make the choice to be happy, patient and kind. "Just imagine."

A Scripture... "A joyful heart is good medicine, but a crushed spirit dries up the bones." ~ Proverbs 17:22

And a Prayer... There is joy in your creation, Father! But sometimes I forget to see it. I trade laughter for tears and encouragement for doubt. There is pain and suffering in this world, Father, but oh, don't let me forget the joy of life. In Jesus's name, Amen

Winding roads, twists, turns
Exit left then sharp turn right
Life roams on its way

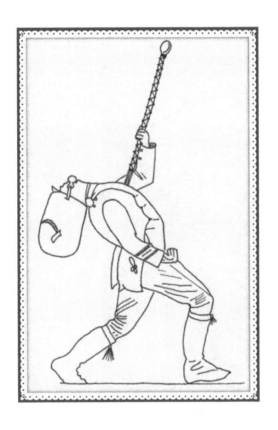

CHAPTER EIGHTEEN

Backward Down the Road of Life

"Take the next left," Lillybelle said.

Annabelle peered through the windshield of their old Volkswagen van. "Are you sure?"

"Of course I'm sure. Do you think I want to get lost?"

"Of course not, Sister." Annabelle put on her blinker. When the light changed to green, she turned onto Richmont Street. "Is the antique store on the left or the right?"

"Left, I think. Sister, what in the world is that coming toward us?"

Annabelle slowed the van. "I do believe it's a parade."

The midmorning sun shined down on three brightly dressed twirlers as they tossed orange, fringed batons in perfect unison. Behind the twirlers, two old-timey prospectors carried a sign that proclaiming, "Dustbowl Days." Behind the prospectors marched the high school band playing with enthusiasm.

Annabelle came to a complete stop.

"Did you see a sign advertising a parade?" Lillybelle asked.

"Of course I didn't see a sign." Annabelle looked around. "A parade would certainly explain all the people standing on the sidewalk."

"Well! If people want to hold a parade, they need to block off the roads."

"I agree, but that doesn't really help us now." Annabelle waved.

"What are you doing?"

"People are waving. I'm just being polite."

"Does nothing embarrass you? While you're being polite, we'd better get out of the way. That parade is getting closer."

"How? All the parking spaces are full."

"Back up?"

"Back up?" Annabelle repeated.

"There's an open space about five cars back."

Annabelle eased the van into reverse. As it moved backward, the crowd clapped and whistled. Annabelle smiled and waved.

Lillybelle shielded her face from the crowd with her hand.

Annabelle backed the van until she could pull into the empty parking spot. With a swirl and flourish, the small parade marched by and continued on its way.

"Did you see those people on the sidewalk?" Lillybelle asked. "They had their phones out. They were taking pictures!"

"Maybe we'll go viral," Annabelle said.

"What?"

"That's when a photo gets shown all over the internet."

"Oh, Lord," Lillybelle said.

Annabelle took it as a prayer. She laughed.

"What is so funny?" Lillybelle demanded.

"When we left the house this morning, did you ever dream we'd end up leading a parade?"

Lillybelle smiled. "No, I guess I didn't."

"Who says life has to be predictable?"

"Not me. At least as long as I live with you!"

"Why, thank you, Sister. That's about the nicest thing you've ever said to me."

A Thought... No matter how hard you try to plan your day, even down to the last perfect minute, you just might end up leading a parade. Life is always full of surprises.

A Scripture... "So do not worry, saying, 'What shall we eat?' or 'What shall we drink?' or 'What shall we wear?'" ~ Matthew 6:31

And a Prayer... Dear Father, I'm not in control. You are. I need to stop worrying, stop trying to make everything go right in life. I trust *You* to see me through. In Jesus' name, Amen

No candy, no sweets
Gosh! Only good-for-you treats
The ULTIMATE trick!

CHAPTER NINETEEN

Trunk or Treat

"The bulletin says the church needs help with 'Trunk or Treat' again this year," Annabelle remarked. She took a sip of ginger tea. "Sounds like so much fun."

"It sounds like a lot of work," Lillybelle replied. She settled into the chair across the kitchen table. "Don't go getting a bee in your bonnet."

Annabelle looked thoughtful. "I haven't heard that expression in years. Where do you think it came from?"

"I don't know. But it always came across as sound advice to me."

"Hmm."

"You're thinking, Sister," Lillybelle accused.

"Yes. Yes I am."

"Well, stop it. We're too old for costumes and all that nonsense. Leave Halloween to the young."

"But wouldn't the van look great decorated as Noah's ark? And we could get Elma and Rita to help."

Lillybelle snorted. "The van's about as old as the ark." She paused to open a can of cat food. With Primrose taken care of, she turned back to her sister. "I'll help on one condition."

"What's that, Sister?"

"We give out healthy treats."

"No candy?"

"Raisins."

Annabelle groaned. "But it's Halloween."

"So, it's okay for kids' teeth to rot on Halloween?"

Annabelle groaned again and muttered, "You are so...so... *you*."

§

The next evening Annabelle pulled the van into the turnabout at the Shady Rest Nursing Home.

"That name would be great on a cemetery gate," Lillybelle grumbled.

"You say that every time, Sister. But I have to agree." Annabelle got out and opened the back door. She helped Elma into the van then handed her Rita's walker. Annabelle pushed, while Lillybelle pulled, their friend into the van. "It's a good thing you weigh less than a bird," Annabelle remarked.

Rita giggled. "I never have been able to gain weight."

Everyone settled, Annabelle climbed back into the driver's seat. "Noah, here we come!"

Rita reached into the bag hanging from her walker and held up some peel and stick pictures. "Look what I found. We can put them in the windows. It'll look like animals peeking out of portholes."

"What a wonderful idea," Annabelle said.

Lillybelle peered at the stickers. "Those *will* come off won't they?"

"Of course, dear," Annabelle said. "They're just like the bells we put on our front windows at Christmas."

Elma patted her rotund bottom and giggled. "You girls don't let me eat too much candy, you hear? It goes straight to my hips."

"Well, you should have no problem this year," Annabelle said. "Lillybelle brought raisins to give out."

"Raisins?" Rita squeaked. "But it's Halloween!"

"Well, little Miss-never-able-to-gain-weight," Lillybelle commented. "America has an obesity problem in case you haven't noticed."

"Humph," Rita said. "Our Lillybelle will be Lillybelle, won't she?"

"What does that mean?" Lillybelle demanded.

"Nothing," Rita replied.

Lillybelle glared.

"I can't wait to decorate," Annabelle soothed.

"Oh, me, too," Elma chimed in. "We're going to turn this van into the cutest little ark anyone's ever seen."

"And when the kids see what we're giving out, they're going to disembark as fast as the animals did after forty days and forty nights of rain," Rita muttered.

"What?" Lillybelle asked.

Rita spoke louder, "When the kids see the decorating, they're going to think they're on a real ark complete with animals."

"I certainly hope so, since that's the look we are going for," Lillybelle replied.

In the church parking lot, the ladies set to work. Rita put up her animal stickers and Elma arranged bales of hay. Annabelle and Lillybelle placed a wooden ramp against the back of the van.

"Delightful!" Elma declared. "And we couldn't have asked for better weather."

"A nice, crisp fall evening," Annabelle agreed. "Don't all the beautiful orange and gold leaves just say fall and Halloween?"

"Yes, they do," Rita agreed. She looked around. "What are we putting the candy, er, raisins in?"

Annabelle held up feed bags. "These!"

"Why, they're as cute as can be," Elma said.

In spite of a marked lack of enthusiasm by three of the decorators, the four women filled the bags with boxes of raisins.

Young Jonathan strolled over carrying a bulging Wallymart bag. He wore a red and white Dr. Seuss hat and green and blue oversized suspenders. Jonathan looked over their van/ark. "Cool!" He held out the bag. "Do you ladies need candy? A lot was donated."

"We brought our own," Annabelle said.

"Actually," Rita said, with a glare at Lillybelle, "we brought raisins."

"But it's Halloween!" Jonathan declared.

"So I've been told," Lillybelle snapped.

The teenager grinned. "I'll bet it was your idea, wasn't it, Miz Lillybelle?"

Lillybelle just sniffed.

"Oh, look," Annabelle exclaimed, "here come the kids."

"Catch you later," Jonathan yelled over his shoulder as he hurried away.

"Don't the little ones look cute?" Elma asked.

"Precious," Annabelle replied.

"I'll be back in just a moment," Lillybelle said. Without waiting for a response, she headed at a brisk trot in the direction of the church building.

"Oh, dear," Annabelle said. "I hope we haven't hurt her feelings about the raisins. Her heart is in the right place."

"Humph," Rita said.

The kids swarmed the van.

"Cool!" a green dragon exclaimed.

"Hey, we get to walk into the ark," a princess said.

One miniature ghost cried, "Look at the camel in the window."

Then a little chipmunk frowned. "Raisins! Where's the candy?"

"Say thank you," his mother instructed.

"Thank you," the chipmunk muttered.

"So thoughtful," his mother told the ladies. "They do get plenty of candy."

Lillybelle returned. She seemed subdued. Annabelle felt sorry about the hard time they'd given her about the raisins.

After about a half hour, Rita whispered, "Have you noticed that we don't seem very popular?"

"Yes," Annabelle agreed. "But for some reason, my sister is the belle of the ball." She moved over next to Lillybelle. "Sister, let me see what's in your feed bag."

"Why?"

"Indulge us," Rita said.

Lillybelle opened her bag.

"Chocolate!" Annabelle exclaimed.

"Lollypops!" Rita shouted.

"Is that banana taffy?" Elma asked.

"What gives?" Annabelle demanded.

Lillybelle had the grace to look sheepish. "For once, I didn't want to be 'that Lillybelle.' I wanted to be the fun one."

Annabelle gave her a hug. "Oh, Sister."

"I'm sorry I made such a fuss," Lillybelle told them.

"Prove it," Rita said. "Give us some candy."

"Of course," Lillybelle said placing a handful of candy in each of their feed bags. "After all, it is Halloween."

A Thought. . . What we perceive as someone's standoffishness, could simply be extreme shyness. Give people a chance to show you who they really are. They might surprise you. Maybe your friend who always wears beige secretly covets red stilettos. ☺

A Scripture. . . *"Do to others as you would have them do to you."* ~ *Luke 6:31*

And a Prayer. . . Help me to give others the benefit of the doubt, Father. When I judge others prematurely, I don't give myself a chance to really know them. In Jesus' name, Amen

My best heels forward
Attitude of my choosing
Creating my world

CHAPTER TWENTY

A Little Praise

Annabelle slowed the ancient VW van. "There's the building."

Lillybelle craned her neck. "Yes, there's the building. But I don't see any parking spots."

"What do you mean? There's one right there."

"You'd have to parallel park," Lillybelle said.

"So?"

"You don't know how to parallel park."

"I most certainly do," Annabelle countered. "I just haven't done it since Bill worked downtown."

"When your husband worked downtown, thongs were still something people wore on their feet."

Annabelle's hoop earrings swayed softly as she eyed the space. "Hush. I've got to concentrate. Now, if I remember right, I pull parallel to the vehicle parked in front, then start turning the wheel as I back up. I should slide right into the space."

"Or take out the rear end of that BMW," Lillybelle remarked.

"You could help, you know."

"How?"

"Get out and direct."

"Oh, very well." Lillybelle opened the door and slid out of the van. "Wait, I need my purse."

"For what?"

"In case you have an accident and I need to call 911."

"How big an accident do you think I'm going to have?"

"Have it your way." Lillybelle smoothed her waved hair and slammed the door in her most ladylike manner. "Okay, begin."

Annabelle carefully put the van in reverse and started backing, turning the wheel ever so slightly.

"Okay. Okay, that's...stop!"

Annabelle slammed on the brake. "Am I close?"

"Only if you plan on adding a little silver to our turquoise van. Not that we'd notice amongst all the other bumps and scratches, but the BMW's owner might."

Annabelle eased the van forward. This time when she backed, she waited a little longer before turning the wheels. Easy...easy...she had...BUMP.

Oh, dear Lord! She'd hit Lillybelle!

"That was the curb," came Lillybelle's calm voice, "in case you were interested. Try again."

Deep breaths. You can do this. Annabelle eased the vehicle forward again then back, turning and straightening. She was in the space, she was...

"Stop!" screeched Lillybelle.

Annabelle hit the brakes. "What?"

"You and that SUV were about to become close personal friends."

"So, what do I need to do now?"

"Nothing, you're in the spot. Now can I get my purse?"

Annabelle let her muscles relax. She'd done it! She reached up and patted herself on the back. "You go, girl!"

"What in the world are you doing?" her sister asked.

"Praising myself for a job well-done."

"Isn't that thinking highly of yourself?"

"I see nothing wrong with giving yourself a little praise now and then."

"Remember," Lillybelle warned, "pride goeth before a fall."

"It has nothing to do with pride," Annabelle protested. "We are so quick to put ourselves down when we fail. I think we should be just as quick to build ourselves up when we succeed."

"You may be right," Lillybelle said. She reached up and patted herself on the back.

"What are you praising yourself for?" Annabelle asked.

"Letting you drive today. I could never have negotiated that parking spot."

"Especially since you don't like to drive."

"Especially so. Aren't I smart?"

A Thought... Praise given for a job well done is deserved, whether it is to others or to self. ~ Mischelle Creager

A Scripture... *"For we are God's handiwork, created in Christ Jesus to do good works, which God prepared in advance for us to do."~* Ephesians 2:10

And a Prayer... Father, I know false modesty is as bad as false vanity, But help me acknowledge when I do well, to realize that I'm a wonderful person. After all, *You* made me! In Jesus' name, Amen

A dusting of white
Bringing the winter of days
In yard and on head

CHAPTER TWENTY-ONE

The Best Is Yet To Be

Lillybelle pulled her shawl tight around her shoulders. Leaning back in her rocking chair, she sighed.

Annabelle glanced up from planning her Sunday class lesson. "Is something wrong, Sister?"

"No." Lillybelle stared into the unlit fireplace. She sighed again.

Annabelle moved her laptop aside. "Come on now, what has you so blue?"

Lillybelle frowned. "You know, I've never understood that expression. Blue is a happy color for me; bluebirds, the sky, and our Primrose's blue eyes. God created lots of wonderful blue things."

"Yes, dear, but..."

Lillybelle sighed again. "I was just thinking about the past."

"And that made you blue, er, sad?"

Lillybelle nodded. "Marriage. Babies. It's all over."

"Dead and gone, are you?"

Lillybelle wagged a finger at her. "Now, there you go poking fun at me. All I'm saying is that the best days are behind us."

"Speak for yourself."

"Oh really? What have you got to look forward to?"

"Well, on Sunday I'm going to teach the Naomi-Ruth class. Then in the afternoon, I plan to take homemade ginger cookies to--"

Lillybelle waved a hand. "Little things, little things. The big moments of our lives have passed. Our babies are all grown and gone."

"And thank goodness! I loved my babies, but I also love seeing what fine adults they've become."

"Colic was hard," her sister mused.

Annabelle wrinkled her nose. "And remember dirty diapers?"

Lillybelle chuckled.

"This is *our* time," Annabelle said. "This is the time God has given us to relax after a lifetime of work."

"Like eating popcorn for dinner and not worrying about setting a bad example."

"Or choosing a restaurant that doesn't have booster seats." Annabelle smiled. "The best is *always* yet to be."

"Yes, Sister, I believe you are right." Lillybelle let her shawl slip from her shoulders and stood.

"Where are you going?" Annabelle asked.

"I'm going to call my daughter-in-law so she can tell me my darling grandson's latest antics. Then I'm going upstairs to put on my pajamas. After that, I'll head for the kitchen to pop some popcorn. And you know what? I may even stay up past 9:00."

"Aren't you the rebel?"

"Don't you ever forget it, Sister."

A Thought... Each new day is a day God has given me. I can exist or live. My choice.

A Scripture... *"Whatever you do, work at it with all your heart, as working for the Lord, not for human masters..."* ~ Colossians 3:23

A prayer... Dear Lord, help me remember that as long as you give me breath, you have a purpose for me. Lead me toward that purpose. In Jesus' name, Amen

Soft little whispers
Creeping tentacles causing
Long-lasting sorrow

CHAPTER TWENTY-TWO

Gossip

"Hand me that tea towel, Sister," Lillybelle said as she moved about the church kitchen. "I'll wipe down the sink and we'll be finished."

Annabelle handed her the towel. "It was nice to see so many ladies here. I think moving the ladies' group luncheon to right after Sunday worship was a good idea."

"Of course it was," Lillybelle said. "It was my idea."

Emma James snorted. "Unfortunately, there's nothing we can do to weed out the riffraff."

"I wasn't aware we had 'riffraff' in church," Annabelle said.

Liddy Sue Arnold laughed. "You are so sweet, Annabelle. You never think badly about anyone."

Lillybelle and Annabelle stared at each other and then at Liddy Sue.

"Whatever are you talking about?" Annabelle asked.

Emma answered, "Imogene Clark, that's who."

"Imogene?" Annabelle wrinkled her forehead. "Is she sick?"

"Hardly," Liddy Sue replied with a snort.

Emma moved a little closer. Everyone leaned in.

We look like vultures ready to dig into road kill, Annabelle thought. But she turned her good ear closer to Emma.

"She turned down the kids collecting canned goods for the needy," Emma reported. "Said she was needy, so she might as well keep her food and cut out the middle man."

"Didn't she just come back from a cruise?" Lillybelle asked.

"She surely did," Liddy Sue said. "But she can't spare a few cans."

Annabelle started when the swinging door opened. A tall young woman came through. She looked close to tears. "I've got the last of the plates," she said in a low voice.

Annabelle touched her cheek, wondering if it was as red as those of the other three women. "Kristen--"

--"I'll just put them here. I've got to go." Head high, Kristen slammed the tray on the metal counter, turned and left the kitchen.

"Do you think she heard?" Emma asked.

"Yes," Lillybelle said softly. "She definitely heard us gossiping about her mother."

Later, standing in the foyer, Annabelle still felt awful. "My heart is so heavy I don't think I can carry it, Sister."

"I know what you mean," Lillybelle replied.

They spotted Kristen coming out of the nursery, her three month old asleep on her shoulder.

"Kristen," Annabelle said, "we are so sorry."

"Oh, don't worry; I'm not mad at you. It's those two gossiping old hens that have me furious."

Annabelle stroked baby Devon's cheek. "We were listening and that's just as bad."

"We are so sorry," Lillybelle added.

"My husband and I paid for that cruise," Kristen burst out. "We gave it to Mom on what would have been her and Dad's fiftieth wedding anniversary."

"I know it must have meant a lot to Imogene," Annabelle said.

"So did the card you sent her," Kristen said. "Mom's always worried about not having enough or being a burden. That's just how she is. She's not stingy though, no matter what those two harpies imply. Why don't they talk about the flowers Mom donated from her garden for the parlor?"

Lillybelle rubbed the younger woman's back. "You're right, dear."

Devon stirred.

"I'd better get going," Kristen said.

The sisters watched her leave.

"Sister, we've *got* to fix this," Annabelle said.

"What do you propose?" Lillybelle asked.

"Well, we were so quick to help spread gossip. Why don't we be just as quick to spread something else?"

"I see where you're going with this," Lillybelle said, "and I know just where to start. Come on." They walked over to a group of women that included Emma and Liddy Sue. "Have you heard?"

Several heads swiveled in their direction.

"Did you know Imogene donated those beautiful flowers in the parlor?"

"Oh, really?" one lady said.

"I was just saying how they brighten up the place," another said.

"I... I think so, too," Emma said with a sheepish smile on her face.

"That's the kind of news we should be spreading," Annabelle said as they walked away.

"Yes, Sister, it is. And it's the kind you and I are going to start spreading from now on. Maybe we'll be trendsetters."

Annabelle laughed. "Well, it's about the only kind of trend we can set."

"But it's a good one."

"Yes, it is."

A Thought. . . If you are the "gossip" carrier, before you spread those germy words, think. Would you say this about your parents, spouse or children? Or even one of your friends? If not, don't spread it about someone else's. ~ Mischelle Creager

A Scripture. . . *"A gossip betrays a confidence; so avoid anyone who talks too much."* ~ Proverbs 20:19

And a Prayer. . . Forgive me for past gossip, Father. Help me to be a trustworthy friend who lifts up instead of tears down. In Jesus' name, Amen

Awake to a dream
A blanket of snow and ice
Winter gone to sleep

CHAPTER TWENTY-THREE

Talking About the Weather

"Winter," Lillybelle moaned, "is cold and dreary. It carries the stillness of death in it." She tightened her shawl around her shoulders and inched her rocker closer to the fire.

"Winter," Annabelle countered, "makes me feel alive." She shaped her mouth into an "O" and blew onto the cold window pane. She drew a heart in the frost created by her breath.

After some silence, Lillybelle whimpered again. "It's so cold. I've forgotten what warmth feels like. I'm afraid I won't make it to warmer weather."

"Winter," Annabelle tried to explain, "is cold outside, but inside it's warm and cozy. What's toastier than sitting beside the fire? What you need is some of my special spiced tea." She hurried to the kitchen, humming to the tune of her bangle bracelets jingling on her arm. She came back carrying two steaming mugs.

"Thank you," Lillybelle said. "You're so good to me, Sister."

Annabelle frowned. "You really are feeling down, aren't you?"

Lillybelle sighed. "Just getting old, Sister, just getting old."

"Getting?"

Lillybelle sighed again.

Settling into a flowered easy chair, Annabelle took a sip of tea. "Should we start planning your funeral?"

121

Her sister looked thoughtful. She finished her tea, straightened her pearls and picked up her knitting. "Actually, winter is a terrible season in which to die. All your friends are snowed in and can't come to your funeral. And the ground is too hard for a proper burial."

"So, winter will be lived through?"

"Yes," said Lillybelle, "I believe it will."

A Thought. . . Have you ever noticed in the Bible everything "comes to pass"? Verses never say, "And it came to stay." Grief passes. Troubles are resolved. God guides us through the winter and into spring.

A Scripture. . . "There is a time for everything, and a season for every activity under the heavens." ~ Ecclesiastes 3:1

And a prayer. . . Dear Lord, help me to enjoy every season, whether it's a physical season or a season of the mind. I need to remember that *You* are the Creator and have a purpose. Please help me see the good in your world and to be *content in any and every situation.* In Jesus' name, Amen

Shifting memories
Come to the front ~ ebb away
Waves crash to the shore

CHAPTER TWENTY-FOUR

An Old Beau

Annabelle squinted at the brightly colored bottle in her hand. "I believe this will do, Sister."

"Shhh," Lillybelle replied.

"We're far too old to be embarrassed about constipation."

"You are never too old to be delicate. But that's not what I'm shushing you about."

Annabelle looked around. "Then what?"

Lillybelle pointed. "Him."

"He looks familiar. Where do we know him from?" Before Annabelle could inquire further, Lillybelle grabbed her arm and yanked her into the next aisle.

"Oh my, that *is* a good price," Annabelle said rubbing her shoulder. "But surely you didn't almost dislocate my arm for a good sale on toilet paper?"

Lillybelle peered around the end of the aisle. "Didn't you recognize him?"

"I didn't have a chance." Annabelle started forward to take her own peek.

"Don't look!"

Annabelle backed up. "Sister, maybe we should find you a nice quiet place to sit."

Lillybelle patted her neatly styled gray hair and smoothed her navy slacks. "I beg your pardon?"

Annabelle chuckled. "Why, Lillybelle Maudine Granger, you're all flushed. Who is that gentleman? Someone from the senior center?"

"It's Martin."

Annabelle frowned. "Martin?"

"Martin!"

"Ahh, *that* Martin. Really? After all this time." Annabelle started for the end of the aisle again.

"Where are you going?" Lillybelle whispered.

"I told you, I didn't get a good look at him."

"I did," Lillybelle said.

"Well?"

"Shorts, black socks, sandals and a comb over!" Lillybelle stated, eyebrow arched.

"Oh."

"Yes. My Harry would never have worn shorts and black socks together."

"Thankfully. Harry's knees were rather knobby."

Lillybelle sniffed. "Like your Phillip was an Adonis."

"I feel we've gotten off track somewhere," Annabelle said.

"You know," Lillybelle mused, "I've sometimes wondered how my life would have turned out if I'd married Martin. He was my high school sweetheart, you know. He was going to be a lawyer."

"I remember," Annabelle said.

"And Martin took me to every musical that came to town. Harry didn't like the theatre."

"True."

Lillybelle nodded sagely. "Life would have been quite different."

A man's voice broke in excitedly. "Lillybelle? Annabelle? I thought I recognized you two!"

Lillybelle smiled. "Why, Martin Sawyer! It's been forever."

He nodded, causing his comb-over to bounce. "You're just as pretty as ever."

Oh my goodness, Annabelle thought, Lillybelle's actually blushing! "Hello, Martin. How have the years treated you?"

"Well, you know I'd planned to go to law school."

Annabelle glanced at her sister who seemed to have lost all ability to speak. "Oh yes, you were going to be the great public defender."

"Well, that didn't pan out. After a couple of years, I realized that career wasn't for me. I dropped out of college and kicked around the country for a few years."

"How exciting!" Annabelle exclaimed.

"It was. Most of the time anyway. I'd travel until I needed to eat and then get a job. I met my dear Rebecca in a little town in the Texas panhandle. We settled down and had seven little Sawyers."

"My, it sounds like you've had a wonderful life!" Annabelle exclaimed.

"I certainly have. Well, it's good to see you ladies again. But I need to run. My oldest daughter is taking me to get new shoes today."

"Good-bye, Martin," Annabelle said.

"Good-bye," Lillybelle echoed.

Annabelle, noticing her sister's frown, asked, "What are you thinking?"

"All these years I've wondered how life as a lawyer's wife would have been. I'd have been Mrs. Vagabond with seven little Sawyers and a husband who wears black socks with sandals."

Annabelle laughed. "That's the problem with rose-colored glasses. They only show the life you *think* you would have lived - without the black socks and sandals."

A Thought... Rose-colored glasses may be pretty, but they aren't accurate. Especially when romanticizing the past or 'what might have been'. Don't get so busy wondering 'what if,' that you forget to take care of the very real present.

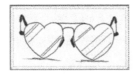

A Scripture.. *"In their hearts humans plan their course, but the Lord establishes their steps."* ~ Proverbs 16:9

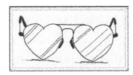

And a Prayer... Dear Lord, I don't want to regret days past, but to rejoice in the things to come. Help me to set my eyes on you and give thanks for all that you've given me. In Jesus' name, Amen

A whisper of wings
And a touch soft as a breeze
Grace personified

CHAPTER TWENTY-FIVE

Talking About Dying

Annabelle shut off the garden hose. "I'm going to die."

Lillybelle pulled off her gardening gloves. "I can pretty much guarantee it. Haven't we had this conversation before? If I remember correctly, you didn't like it when I spoke of dying."

"That was because you were depressed. About the weather, I believe. However, I'm not depressed. I'm simply stating a fact."

"What made you think about death?" Lillybelle asked as they carried the gardening supplies to the tool shed.

"The flowers we just planted. What wonderful hues. Tell me, do you think angel's haloes only come in gold? I'd love a purple one."

"You can't redecorate heaven."

"I don't want to redecorate it. But a lavender robe would go wonderfully with my purple halo, don't you think?"

Lillybelle snorted. "I can hear it now, 'God, I have some ideas...'"

"Do you think He'd mind purple tinted clouds?"

A Thought... I don't know about you, but I have trouble imagining perfection. My insecurities get in the way. But I have faith that heaven will be worth everything I've endured in this imperfect life. I hope to see you there!

A Scripture... *"My Father's house has many rooms; if that were not so, would I have told you that I am going there to prepare a place for you?"* ~ John 14:2

And a Prayer... Father, even though I know there's no pain or heartache in your kingdom, death scares me. I pray that you strengthen my faith, Father. I know Jesus has prepared a perfect place for me. Thank you, Father! In Jesus' name, Amen

Outward beauty is
Illusive and short lasting
Inward beauty lasts

~ Robin Miley Totten

CHAPTER TWENTY-SIX

Sharing Beauty Secrets

"**I** don't think I wear the right bra," Annabelle said. "According to this commercial, I should have more uplift."

Lillybelle shook her head. "Sister dear, after a certain age, it sags... make peace with it."

§

One infomercial later...

"I wasn't aware," said Lillybelle, "duck lips were so in style."

"I think they're supposed to be sexy," Annabelle said.

"Oh."

§

A talk show later...

"Since when did smiling become something only old people do?" Lillybelle asked.

"Since wrinkles were outlawed," Annabelle replied. "You know, I don't believe that woman can move her face."

§

After a commercial for lash extensions...

"I will be one of those rarest of rare creatures," Annabelle declared. "A totally natural woman."

"Well, 'totally natural woman,'" her sister replied, "Put a rinse in your hair, slap some moisturizer on your face, and buy a good bra. And please be quiet. This nice lady on television is going to tell us how we can be desirable to men just by using her perfume."

A Thought. . . What if we had a special mirror that showed us what's important to God? Would we see a heart that is too small, a blemish caused by a wayward tongue, feet that hurry to spread gossip? What would you change about yourself if you saw your true reflection? ~ Mischelle Creager

A Scripture. . . *"Therefore we do not lose heart. Though outwardly we are wasting away, yet inwardly we are being renewed day by day."* ~ 2 Corinthians 4:16

And a Prayer... Lord, there are so many things that pull me to focus on my outer beauty. Please help me this week to focus on my inner self, to make sure it is beautiful in your eyes. In Jesus' name, Amen

Wispy, shimmery
Bubbles floating to the sky
Fragile as a soul

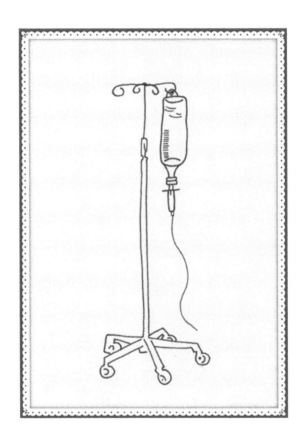

CHAPTER TWENTY-SEVEN

A Little Understanding

Lillybelle opened her eyes. "I expected heaven to be more pearly white and less beige."

Annabelle leaned over her. "You're in the hospital, Sister, not heaven. And this is a vast improvement over the pea green walls of the emergency room."

Lillybelle tried to move her arm, but found tubes blocking her way. "What happened?"

"You had a heart attack, dear. Remember?"

Lillybelle nodded. "I thought maybe it was the pickled herring, but…"

"It wasn't," her sister told her. "How are you feeling?"

"Tired. Have you seen my doctor?"

"He stopped by about a half-hour ago. He assured me it was a very mild heart attack."

"So I can go home?"

"No, dear, I'm afraid not quite yet. Are you okay?"

"You mean aside from the heart attack? Yes."

"Can I get you anything?"

"No… I think I'll go back to sleep."

§

Lillybelle opened her eyes.

139

The preacher smiled down at her. "Good morning, Lillybelle. How are you doing?"

"Aside from the heart attack, fine. Can I do anything for you, Brother Ames?"

He looked a little surprised. "Well, uh, I actually came by to see if I could do anything for you." He touched her arm. "Are there any fears you'd like to address?"

"Fears? No, I know the Lord is watching out for me."

"Would you like me to say a prayer?"

"That would be nice. We've been needing rain. Ask God for that."

§

"And how are you feeling?" Doctor Bennett asked when Lillybelle next opened her eyes.

"Really, Doctor. You of all people should know I just had a heart attack. Other than that, I'm fine."

"Of course," he soothed.

Annabelle attempted to fluff her sister's pillow.

"Sister," Lillybelle told her, "you're hovering. Can I go home?" she asked the doctor.

"Not quite yet. We want to keep you another night."

"I suppose you're going to give me more pills. I've already built a miniature wall in the bathroom with the ones I'm taking."

He patted her arm. "Part of getting old, I'm afraid." He left the room.

"Can I get you anything, Sister?" Annabelle asked, trying to make the question sound like she wasn't hovering.

"My Bible would be nice."

"It's right here."

§

Lillybelle opened her eyes. She could hear movement in the hall-way, but her room was dark. "Lord," she whispered, "I know I'm in your hands."

Annabelle sat up in the sleep chair. "Did you say something?"

"Who me?"

Annabelle scrambled to her feet. "Are you hurting? Do you need me to call a nurse?"

"No..."

"Then what?"

"I... I was just telling the Lord that I know He's going to take care of me."

Annabelle sat on the side of the bed and put an arm around her sister. "You know it's okay, don't you?"

"Yes. A little medication and I'll be right as rain."

"No, I mean it's okay to be afraid. God will understand."

"At seventy-two, I'm supposed to be prepared to meet my Maker."

"But if you aren't quite ready to go today, it's okay. God made us to love this life He's given us. Even as He's taught us to be prepared for heaven."

Two tears rolled down Lillybelle's wrinkled cheeks. "But..."

Her sister hugged her tight.

"Dear God," Lillybelle whispered, "I'm so afraid."

A Thought. . . I'm scared. I don't understand. I'm angry. There's no situation we can't take to God. He won't be offended. He promises to be there for us whenever we are afraid or hurting or when we don't even know how to pray. Just start talking. I promise He's listening.

A Scripture. . . *"Those who know your name will trust in you, for you, LORD, have never forsaken those who seek you."* ~ Psalm 9:10

And a Prayer. . . Dear God, when my fear surfaces, help me see it as an opportunity to turn my problems over to you. In Jesus' name, Amen

Kisses on ouches
Peanut butter and jelly
Sensible clog life

The Tattoo

"Sometimes change is good," Annabelle stated. "It's important to shake yourself out of your comfort zone."

Lillybelle peered up from her crochet. "Did you have a certain change in mind?"

"A tattoo."

Startled, Lillybelle dropped her yarn. It rolled onto the floor where Primrose pounced on it. "A what?"

"You heard me." Annabelle touched her left wrist. "A little daisy right there."

"I'd accuse you of having a blonde moment, but you haven't been blonde in 30 years," Lillybelle replied as she rescued her yarn. "What will people think?"

"Oh, hush. It's not like I plan on an entire mural scrawled down my arm. Just a tasteful, little daisy."

"Mercy me," was all Lillybelle could say.

§

"Whatever happened to getting that tattoo?" Lillybelle asked about a week later as she cleared the table.

Annabelle sighed. "I'd hoped you'd forgotten all about my silly notion." She put a glass in the dishwasher and reached for the plates in Lillybelle's hand.

"What made you to come to your senses?"

"Well, I decided that maybe I'm a little too old to be getting a tattoo."

"I'm not." With a flourish, Lillybelle held up her left wrist. A tiny, purple butterfly adorned it.

"Oh, my goodness," Annabelle exclaimed.

Lillybelle barely caught the dish that slipped through her sister's suddenly lax fingers.

Annabelle gasped. "I can't believe you, of all people, got a tattoo." She reached back and fumbled for a chair.

Lillybelle set the plate on the counter and pulled out the chair. "Do you need to breathe into a paper bag?"

Annabelle shook her head. "I chickened out, and *you* did it."

Lillybelle sat beside her sister and held out her wrist. "Well, not exactly. It's not permanent."

Annabelle peered closer. "You can't tell."

"I've been assured it will fade away."

"No needles?"

"Not a one."

Annabelle chuckled. "So, tell me, Sister. Why a tattoo?"

"Because you were right. We do need to occasionally shake ourselves out of our comfort zone."

"But not permanently?"

"I'm not the same person I was twenty years ago. How do I know what person I will be in twenty more?"

"You'll be ninety-two."

"Yes, and at ninety-two, I might not want a butterfly tattoo. I might prefer a rose."

"Very smart, Sister."

"Thank you. Now, how about we get you that daisy tattoo?"

"I think that's a fine idea--as long as no needles are involved."

A Thought. . . What's life without a little drama? Not the kind of drama that hurts feelings and causes pain, but the kind that comes with taking a chance. Maybe today is the day to say yes. Not even a big change, but a small one... a baby step. It might be fun!

A Scripture. . . "I praise you because I am fearfully and wonderfully made, your works are wonderful, I know that full well." ~ Psalm 139:14

And a prayer. . . Dear Father, as long as I stay in Your will, help me to occasionally take a chance. Help me to fully explore this life you've given me. In Jesus' name, Amen

A coat of fresh snow
Lies quietly on the grass
Waiting for children

~ Una Belle Townsend (the original "belle" in my life ☺)

CHAPTER TWENTY-NINE

Getting in the Spirit

"It's rather chilly out," Annabelle remarked.

"Jack Frost is definitely nipping at noses today," Lillybelle agreed. She took a sip of tea from a mug decorated with snowflakes and snuggled deeper into her afghan. "It certainly feels like the Christmas season."

"It would be a good day to stay in," Annabelle said. "Where are those car keys?"

"On their hook," Lillybelle replied. "Where are you going? I thought you'd finished all your holiday shopping."

"I have. *We* are going to the soup kitchen."

Lillybelle frowned. "I thought we weren't going to sign up this year. Did I forget? Did you forget to mark it on the calendar?"

"We weren't. And no to both your other questions. But I got an email from Mary Sue this morning. She said they were low on volunteers."

Lillybelle put down her tea and rubbed a leg. "I can't imagine standing all evening."

Annabelle dropped into a chair. "To tell the truth, I can't either."

"You know, Sister, standing for hours serving soup is really a young person's activity."

"I agree, Sister. Of course…"

"Of course what?"

"The young are all so busy. Parents with little children are getting ready for Santa's visit; college students are visiting friends they haven't seen all semester. It's us old people with the free time."

Lillybelle folded her afghan and laid it across the arm of the rocker. "I know, I know." She reluctantly slipped her feet out of her fuzzy slippers and into her boots.

"It *is* fun to see the children's faces when Santa Claus shows up at the end of the meal," Annabelle mused.

"That's true."

"And I bet no one will mind if we sit on chairs while we serve."

Lillybelle put on her hat. "Again, you're right. You know what?"

"What?" Annabelle slipped on red mittens with white reindeer embroidered on them.

"You know how they're always talking about old people forced out to pasture?"

"Yes."

Lillybelle opened the door to the garage. "I think it's a myth."

"Merry Christmas, Lillybelle."

"Merry Christmas, Annabelle."

A Thought... Go ahead, check your body—the back of your heel, the back of your hand, the back—well--the back of whatever. Is there a date stamped "Free to stop helping, free to live for your own pleasure, free to not care about others at age ___?" If you don't find one, keep on helping, teaching, being an example. Your efforts will be blessed. ~ Mischelle Creager

A Scripture... *"Share with the Lord's people who are in need. Practice hospitality."*~ Romans 12:13

And a Prayer... No matter my age, there is something I can do for You, Father. Help me remember there is always something I can do for my brothers and sisters in Christ. I am not useless unless I let myself be useless. In Jesus' name, Amen

Trinkets of our lives
Silly and sentimental
The treasures of time

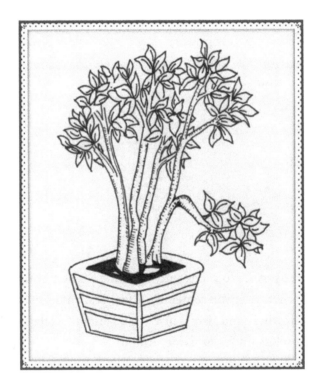

CHAPTER THIRTY

Dirty Socks

Annabelle watched Chelsea Waynesboro catch one child by the arm and another by the hem of her shirt. "Stand still," the young mother ordered.

Annabelle chuckled. "Oh, I remember those days."

"Yes," Liddy Sue said. "I do miss little ones."

Chelsea straightened a ponytail and pointed the girls toward the children's wing. "Go to Sunday school."

"Yes, ma'am," Charlotte, the older of the two, said with a giggle.

"And no running," Chelsea shouted as the two girls raced down the hall. She sighed.

Annabelle patted her on the arm. "You are so lucky."

Liddy Sue added, "Such adorable little girls."

"Yeah, well Adorable Number One tried to stick a fork in Adorable Number Two's hand this morning because she was taking the last piece of bacon," Chelsea said. "To get even, Adorable Number Two licked it and put it back on the plate."

Liddy Sue blinked. "When my girls were little, we felt it important to discipline."

"I took away their TV privileges and they're going to bed an hour earlier tonight. Any other suggestions?"

"Um, why no." Liddy Sue hurried off.

Annabelle laughed. "Oh dear, I think you shocked her. Kids will be kids, won't they? Just don't forget to enjoy them while they're still young. They grow up so fast."

"I'll try and remember that," Chelsea muttered as Annabelle headed to class.

"Humph," came a voice from behind the fichus tree. "Platitudes aren't quite as helpful as we think they are."

"Miss Lillybelle," Chelsea exclaimed. "What are you doing sitting behind that potted plant?"

"Hiding. Come join me."

Chelsea joined her. "I'll bet your kids never acted like that. You never had to pull them apart, or have them finish dressing in the car."

Lillybelle chuckled. "Let me tell you a secret. Now, you have to remember, this was back in the old days when wives were supposed to keep a perfect house, cook dinner every night and take care of the kids. Well, one Sunday morning, I was running around trying to find hair barrettes while getting my slowpoke, Michael, to finish his eggs. My husband had a crisis. He couldn't find any clean socks. Well, he couldn't find any clean socks because my son had spilled a gallon of milk in the laundry basket the night before and I hadn't gotten around to redoing the load. Anyway, to make a long story short, I told my husband to get a pair out of the dirty clothes and wear them. And he did."

Chelsea laughed. "I don't believe it."

Lillybelle crossed her heart and grinned. "It's true."

"You just made my day. I mean, I thought you were perfect."

"The only perfect human being that ever lived was smart enough never to have children. I'm glad to have obliged, dear. Remember, it's our little secret. We wouldn't want it to get out that I'm not perfect."

A Thought... Everyone is perfect. Except me. At least that's how I feel a lot of the time. And I bet I'm not the only one who feels that way. Maybe I can help someone else realize it's okay to have "off days" (weeks!). Let's all be imperfect together!

A Scripture... *"Likewise, teach the older women to be reverent in the way they live, not to be slanderers or addicted to much wine, but to teach what is good."* ~ *Titus 2:3*

And a Prayer... Oh, dear Father, help me to remember what it was like to be a new mother. And help me to pass on not only advice (when asked!), but compassion and humor. In Jesus' name, Amen

Immortal mortal
Physical flesh turns to dust
The soul eternal

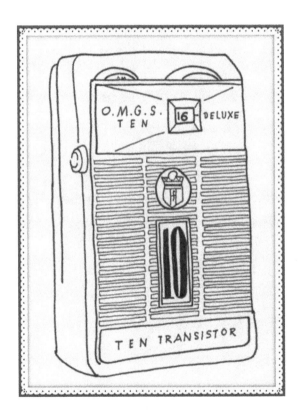

CHAPTER THIRTY-ONE

You Can't Get Rid of Me!

"Stay awake, you old fool," Annabelle muttered. She wasn't in the habit of calling herself a fool, but this time it applied. The cabin had heat. There had been no need to try and chop wood. She reached back and gently touched the back of her head. It was tender, but thank God the bleeding had stopped.

Waves of nausea followed an urge to curl up and go to sleep.

"Stand up and walk," Annabelle ordered herself. But standing made her head hurt worse. "It's all Lillybelle's fault," she complained to the coatrack. "We were supposed to come clean out this old cabin together. But she was afraid an ice storm might hit. Lillybelle was right. Now I'll never hear the end of it."

She eased herself onto the edge of a kitchen chair, trying not to get too comfortable. She needed someone to talk to, someone to help keep her awake. The urgent care station would be checking in again soon. Her eyes sought out the kitchen timer. Had it really been forty-five minutes? The station was supposed to check on her every thirty minutes.

Annabelle checked her cell phone. It was dead. Lillybelle always remembered the charger. This was her fault, too!

"At least the radio will be noise," Annabelle told the coatrack. She turned the radio on in spite of the fact the only station it got was from a local agricultural college specializing in farm reports. Sure enough, she was going to learn more about pigs than she ever wanted to know.

"Annabelle?"

Annabelle blinked. Were they talking about a pig named Annabelle? Could a concussion, and she was sure she had one, play tricks on your mind?

Lillybelle's voice came through the radio. "Annabelle, it's me. You old fool, I told you not to go up to the cabin today. You could be in town right now at that cozy B & B. But no, you had to go up the hill."

Tears sprang to Annabelle's eyes. "Sister, you knew I'd turn the radio on."

"I know you can't stand silence. I'll bet you're sitting there blaming me, aren't you?" Lillybelle continued. "That's okay. The paramedics will be there soon. They wouldn't let me ride with them because of the ice, but this nice young man at the radio station let me borrow it for a moment. We'll be together soon, Sister. You know you can't lose me. God and me, you can't lose either of us."

Annabelle closed her eyes. "Thank you." It was all she needed to say. Lillybelle and God understood.

A Thought... If you were the only person on earth who believed in Him, Jesus still would have died for you. You are that important. Remember, you can't lose God. He's always just a prayer away.

A Scripture... *"And surely I am with you always, to the very end of the age."* ~ Matthew 28:20b

And a Prayer... Dear Father, help me to believe in the certainty of You, that You keep Your word, and Your word says You will always be with me. Help me, Oh Lord, not to leave or forsake You. Because I know that's the only way I can lose You. In Jesus' name, Amen

ABOUT THE AUTHOR

Susan York Meyers is the author of two chapter books, *Callie and the Stepmother* and *The Princess and the Pee*, as well as two picture books, *Grrr...Night!* and *The Mystery of the Red Mitten*. *Grrr...Night!* received the 2015 Creative Women of Okla-homa Award for writing.

Susan lives in Oklahoma with her husband, her son, and Kira the dog, who thinks she's people.

For information on speaking engagements, visit Susan's website at **susanameyers.com.**

ABOUT THE ILLUSTRATOR

Acacia Anthis is a self-taught pen & ink artist.

She works for a non-profit organization, but to keep her anxiety low and her creativity alive, she indulges in artsy things. When not in her studio, Anthis loves being outdoors, conquering new things, volunteering, and spending time with friends and family.

CPSIA information can be obtained
at www.ICGtesting.com
Printed in the USA
LVHW010533291118
598633LV00018B/1804/P